PATRICIA HEATON'S
Food for Family and Friends

PATRICIA HEATON'S

Food for Family and Friends

100 FAVORITE RECIPES FOR A BUSY, HAPPY LIFE

PATRICIA HEATON

PHOTOGRAPHY BY ED ANDERSON

WILLIAM MORROW

An Imprint of HarperCollins*Publishers*

HarperCollins books may be purchased for educational, business, or
sales promotional use. For information, please email the Special Markets
Department at SPsales@harpercollins.com.

FIRST EDITION

Designed by Renata De Oliveira
Photography by Ed Anderson

Library of Congress Cataloging-in-Publication Data has been applied for.

ISBN 978-0-06-267244-5
ISBN 978-0-06-285102-4 (B&N Signed Edition)
ISBN 978-0-06-285103-1 (BAM Signed Edition)
ISBN 978-0-06-285104-8 (BJs Signed Edition)

18 19 20 21 22   QDG   10 9 8 7 6 5 4 3 2 1

I dedicate this book to all those things that feed me: my faith, my family, and my friends

Contents

Introduction

I'm an extrovert.

I know this because my son had to take a personality test and I figured, as a responsible mother, I'd do it with him. But secretly, I wanted to make sure I'd chosen the right profession because, well, maybe two decades of network television was simply a warm-up for a quiet career in a laboratory, right? Maybe I was destined to be a botanist! Maybe I'm in the wrong life . . .

It sounds so *peaceful*, being a botanist.

But no. My Nobel Prize got stuck in Stockholm when the test declared me an extrovert, which explains my uncontrollable urge to dress up in costumes and play silly characters, but it also means that I like people; I feel activated and energized when I'm with others.

Well, I could have told them *that*.

My whole life, I've enjoyed all matter of mingling, chitchatting, and general late-night schmoozing. And I especially like feeding people. There's nothing better than seeing a loved one close his eyes and exhale that this-is-really-*good* sigh as he tastes a bite of food I've cooked. (I use "he" only because I'm surrounded by bearers of the Y chromosome in my household, but more

on that later.) There's a real gut-level joy in feeding someone.

And I can get philosophical on the topic: I think bringing people together to eat is profoundly important. Whether it's with family or friends, when we sit down (or stand up . . . cocktails and canapés, anyone?) and feast in one another's company, we are doing more than storing calories; we are strengthening the fabric of our *community*. Humanity even. And yes, I'm getting deep here because, although I love some gossipy small talk as much as the next person, I also relish some spirit-y big talk every once in a while, too, so I hope you can indulge me.

And indulge yourself! I wrote this book to help you serve up fantastic, mouthwatering dishes, so whether you're cooking to pamper Number One (Earl Grey Flourless Chocolate Cake), nourish your family (Hearty Lamb Stew), or throw a full-blown, fancy-schmancy soiree (Bite-Size Crab Cakes with Lemon Aioli), I've got you covered. My goal is to offer you inspiration, practical tips, and recipes that will stay in your family for generations. Because, of all the people in my life, my fans hold a special (and very big) place in my heart. Without

you guys, I'm just an unemployed actress pretending to be a strip of bacon on the floor of some acting class, and that's not pretty.

Or kosher.

So *thank you* for all your support over the years; for laughing and joining in on the fun—whether it was with *Everybody Loves Raymond*, or *The Middle*, or my cooking show, *Patricia Heaton Parties*. You could have thrown tomatoes, but instead, you threw Emmys. This book is one way of returning that affection.

Remember, to feed is to love. When we cook, we stir our hearts into the food, and that's powerful stuff. Words are great, and we can say "I love you" 'til we're blue in the face, but sometimes it's the meatball that does the talking. Cooking is my chance to bond with my friends, love my husband, and to communicate with my teenage sons when they don't feel like mumbling at Mom. Which is often.

And when they bite down, close their eyes, and sigh, I feel like they're loving me right back. That's a great gift.

Although diamonds are better. Let's be honest.

part one
My Food Story

Before we dive into the recipes and my philosophy on feeding family and friends, I'd like to give you some of my background vis-à-vis nourishment. Like yours, my relationship with food snuck in before my earliest memories, and the foods I ate were intricately woven into the fabric of my life.

As we all know, eating offers more than good tastes and full bellies; it evokes family, places, and distinct times of our lives. Food gets under our skin because it actually gets *inside* our skin; it's an intimate thing!

So as you read my story, I encourage you to let your own food memories bubble up.

The Herd

I was recently at a swanky L.A. bar with Eden Sher, who plays my daughter, Sue, on *The Middle*. We were laughing and talking shop over dinner when the bartender started hovering a bit. This sort of thing happens when you're a celebrity; people get nervous and kind of hover as they muster up the courage to ask for an autograph. It's sweet, and happens all the time since I won my third Emmy (which—you might notice—I try to work into every conversation). The poor thing was holding a cocktail napkin for my John Hancock, so I smiled and reached into my purse for my special autograph pen, when he blurted, "I think we're second cousins!"

Awkward.

For many people, this kind of thing might be unusual, or even exciting, but for me, it's just another day as a member of the Hurd clan. My mother was one of *fifteen* children, and I'm the forty-ninth grandchild on my mother's side of the family. True story: My grandmother was named United States Catholic Mother of the Year and was awarded a medal by His Holiness, Pope Pius XXII! With more than a hundred first and second cousins in our crew, you can imagine that the statistical probability of Hurd family mashups is high.

I steadied myself with a sip of my drink, reassessing the situation. "Although I'm inclined to believe you . . ."—I looked into his eyes, now weirdly resembling my brother's, as I issued him the Hurd Family Challenge— "do you have any *proof?*"

Out came the wallet and, sure enough, he presented me with a tattered photo of a bunch of kids surrounding a man I recognized as my uncle Tom. Pointing to the same man, the bartender announced, affectionately, "That's my grandpa Tom." He looked up for my reaction, and I smiled, discreetly dropped my autograph pen, and went in for a big hug with my newly discovered kin. Suddenly I was no longer an actress, let alone a celebrity, in this crazy town called Hollywood. I was just a Hurd, with a fellow member of the Hurd herd. And it felt fantastic.

Bay Village

The Hurds began their American chapter in Ohio—by way of Connecticut—where they met the Heatons, and where I was born in the late 1950s (no need to do the math). All this procreating took place in a suburb of Cleveland called Bay Village. It was the kind of place that people say doesn't exist anymore: As kids, we rode our bikes in the neighborhood until the streetlamps went on and our mothers would stand behind screen doors, yelling for us to come home "right this minute!" or we'd be sorry. No one worried about crime, or terrorism, and the world hadn't even heard of climate change. Families made weekly pilgrimages to the Dairy Queen for Dilly bars, and chummy neighbors threw potlucks with cheesy casseroles and marshmallow-topped whatevers.

Seriously, it was frickin' Mayberry.

Our little town was made up of hardworking folks who didn't have a lot of extra money lying around, and my family was no exception. With five kids in the fold, the purse strings were cinched tight. But penny-pinching didn't stop my mother from dreaming about bigger and better things, especially when it came to dinner.

Arriving home from school, I would find her parked in front of the TV, watching Julia Child and fervently taking notes on how to make the perfect soufflé or boeuf bourguignon.

Bless her. She tried.

Although this scene smacks of domestic devotion, my mother was actually a tomboy type who wore no makeup and preferred reading the philosopher-priest Pierre Teilhard de Chardin to peeling potatoes. An intellectual, deeply into theology and social politics, she was *not* a natural homemaker; she was on top of the *spiritual* housekeeping by going to mass every day.

So perhaps it's no surprise that her Julia Child studies never seemed to translate to Herculean efforts in the kitchen. I present to you the seven meals my mother cooked unfailingly for our stable:

1. Meat loaf
2. Spaghetti and meatballs
3. Chicken
4. Pork chops
5. Burgers
6. Fish sticks (Fridays)
7. Pot roast

'Nuff said.

But what my mother lacked in creativity, she certainly made up for in love; every December, she'd pull out her rolling pin and cookie cutters so we could all bake a huge batch of sugar cookies—some in the shape of stars, and bells, and Christmas trees; others were just weird kid creations. No matter how crazy it got, Mom would just laugh and let us have at it. Covered in flour and sticky with icing, my favorite part was placing those little edible silver balls onto the frosted cookies while she watched. They seemed to sparkle up the whole house.

And like all mothers were instructed to do, she'd make a yearly offering to our school's bake sale, contributing perfectly baked brownies from the box. And although I do my best to let go of these things, one year my sister Alice tried her hand at baking with a chocolate-frosted pound cake. It never made it to the bake sale, however, because she chucked it at my head, knocking me into the cinderblock wall in our basement—that thing weighed *waaaaaaay* more than a pound!

But I digress.

When it came to entertaining, my mother upped her game considerably; the fine tablecloth would come out, along with the fancy napkins, and I was allowed to polish the silverware and the dining room table—jobs I loved. Mom would cook a pot roast or chicken; it was never anything exotic or fancy, but it was served with grace and style.

Dad was a sportswriter, so our dinner guests were often other journalists from the paper, or the coaches of the Cleveland sports teams. Of course, Mom ordered us to "skedaddle!" from the grown-up table, but we'd perch at the stop of the stairs in our pajamas, listening to the laughter and the clinking of glasses. As a little actress, attracted to all kinds of fantasy things, I found these evenings exciting and glamorous.

And it didn't last forever. Downer alert: This magical childhood ended when, in 1971, my mother died of a brain aneurysm. I was twelve, and the second youngest in the family. We were devastated, obviously, and it's taken me a long time to make peace with it. I've sent my therapist's kid to college three times.

But death—as jarring and painful as it can be—doesn't stop the lives of others, and my bewildered father was suddenly responsible for the care and feeding of our clan. It would be a tidy story indeed if I told you that he painstakingly pored over Mom's unused Julia Child notes and reproduced sole meunière and ratatouille to perfection, wouldn't it?

The reality is that we ate beans on buttered bread and Kraft spreadable Cheddar sandwiches for lunch (both still two of my favorite meals when I'm feeling nostalgic). Jell-O molds, Pop-Tarts, cream of mushroom this, and canned that. All washed down with Tang. This was my entire world, gastronomically speaking. But hey, it was the Midwest, in the seventies, and all that processed food made me who I am.

New York

After my stint at Ohio State University (where my job as a Faculty Club waitress taught me how to fold a napkin into a fleur-de-lis—who says kids don't learn anything in college?), I packed up my hopes, dreams, and curling iron and moved to New York City. It was 1980 and I was all of twenty-two.

Funny thing, though, struggling actresses don't tend to get rich dragging themselves to early-morning auditions for shoe commercials while waiting tables on the side, so I lived on Grape-Nuts and yogurt for breakfast.

And lunch.

And dinner.

When I ventured out, my budget allowed for seventy-five-cent, New York–style pizza slices. I sprinkled those babies with oregano and chili flakes and the carbs would light up my brain's pleasure centers like a Christmas tree. The hot grease and cheese ran down my chin and glopped onto the flimsy white paper plate, so I had to eat fast or suffer the messy consequences.

And for dessert? A famous chocolate egg cream, the pride of Brooklyn. Containing neither eggs nor cream, this syrupy-milky-seltzer-y concoction came in a paper cone, nestled in a stainless steel holder made for lifting to the lips. A polite glug-glug of an egg cream made the perfect chaser to my New York slice. Classy.

When I had some cash, late-night Chinese delivery was my savior after a long day, and the guy manning the phone would automatically recite my order after hearing my hello: "Hot and sour soup. Steam pork dumpling. Sesame noodle. Half an hour. Five dollar."

Mmm . . . those cool sesame noodles, served with crunchy, thinly sliced cucumber,

were heaven on those sticky summer nights when, too poor for air conditioning, I'd slap a wet washcloth around my neck and try not to move.

Meanwhile, I'd gotten a morning room-service shift at the swanky Parker Meridien hotel, although I was constantly slowed down by the kitchen's platter of hot, buttery croissants—the ones that stretched teasingly when pulled apart, showering crisp, golden flakes of pastry onto my ever-so-sexy polyester uniform.

But I was sure to wipe myself clean before knocking on a guest's door, because I never knew who had ordered that café au lait—John Denver, Dustin Hoffman, or John Cougar Mellencamp (or John Cougar Underpants, as I liked to call him. Yes, John, I could see you!).

It was in New York, the quintessential global city, that I was introduced to empanadas. I became quite the connoisseur, sampling my way through chorizo and cheese, pickled onion and pork, and picadillo and potato.

Going out with friends, I tried—and fell in love with—sushi. It was also in Manhattan that I got a taste of other fancy foods that I'd never tried in Cleveland, like Brie and quiche and fondue. Ooh-la-la. I was growing up.

As that newly minted grown-up, I also tried my hand at throwing parties. I was living in a tiny studio apartment in the Meatpacking District (a sublet from one of my hundred cousins), and I decided that it would be the perfect place to throw a surprise birthday party for my older brother,

Michael. However, being an actress and not a logician, I hadn't considered that there was no real place to hide in a one-room studio apartment. So, in order to maintain the "surprise" element of the party . . . I stuffed everyone into the bathroom! Alas, my first Martha Stewart moment involved packing thirty of my brother's friends into the toilet like clowns into a Volkswagen.

Resourceful, no?

At the appointed hour, Michael arrived and, within seconds, the bathroom door flew open, unraveling a knot of sweaty friends yelling "Surprise!!!" He was delighted. We were young and fun was cheap.

Sigh.

As cheap as the sound system: a yellow Sony Walkman. For my millennial readers, a Walkman is a rectangular tape player (ask your parents what a tape is) about the size of a sandwich, and it was the granddaddy of the iPod. Back when my generation was hip, we filled the New York streets and subways wearing our not-very-comfortable headphones, tuning out the city, and turning up the volume on the Commodores. And although Walkmans were generally used with headphones, I had ingeniously purchased two tiny speakers on Fourteenth Street (for eight bucks) that I plugged directly into mine, so we could all dance to Michael Jackson and Hall & Oates. Voilà! Instant entertainment center.

I don't think I even cooked that night, because my tiny NYC kitchen was pretty much useless. For me, the beginning of the evening was a blur of bottles, chips, and various dips, after which we all went out for a proper dinner. But everybody totally went with it. I'd thrown my first come-as-you-are, BYOB party, and we'd had a great time.

I sometimes reflect on that night when I'm throwing fancier, more sophisticated parties these days. It reminds me not to worry too much about how everything looks or ends up tasting. Sure, it's nice when it all turns out perfectly, but we managed to have such a good time that night with practically no money, very little food, and the badly amplified squeals of my little sound system. It helps me to remember that it's really about getting people together and just having fun.

It's the spirit that counts.

My hostessing successes notwithstanding, New York was beginning to beat me. After nine years, what had begun as hope and excitement was morphing into cynicism and fatigue. Although I'd booked a few commercials (one with Jason Alexander!) and had lunched with George Steinbrenner (thanks, Dad), pursuing the dream in Manhattan was losing its charm. So I did what many hungry actors do—I moved to L.A., where yet another chapter in my life began.

The City of Angels

Los Angeles. The first thing I noticed was the sky. Vast, clear, and perfectly blue, L.A.'s sky instantly swept away all the New York tension I'd been carrying around inside of me. My shoulders relaxed, and I took a breath so deep I almost inhaled the Pacific.

And the sun—the ridiculously bright sun of Los Angeles—made even the garbage cans sparkle. Whereas New Yorkers are hurried and grumpy, the sunshine made Angelenos seemed relaxed, content, even bordering on spaced out. It was nice to stop bracing for battle.

Although New York will always hold a special place in my heart, it was in L.A. that things really started happening for me: My British boyfriend, David, proposed on one knee, ring in box (jolly good, old chap!), and in short order we were married and embarked upon our multidecade experiment in perfect, domestic bliss.

Ahem.

But marriages don't unfold in decades. Marriages take place, as the alcoholics say, one day at a time. And what do both people in a marriage do every day?

No, not that. They *eat.*

So it didn't take long before my laissez-faire singleton lifestyle bumped up against David's matrimonial assumption that I would do the cooking for us. We had never actually discussed it, but suddenly one night he queried, "What are we having for dinner?"

In the most annoying British accent.

Remember, I had been a single actress, living like a monologue-memorizing bohemian since college, and suddenly this man was asking what I—his little wifey—was planning to rustle up in the kitchen that night.

I had no idea. It was like the worst audition of my life.

Fast forward: I adjusted. More than adjusted, mind you. I figured out the cooking thing (including some British favorites)—one meal at a time—while giving birth to, and caring for, four boys. All while working on *Everybody Loves Raymond*!

A minor miracle, really.

We will get into the details of juggling babies, toddlers, Emmys, and frying pans, but suffice it to say, we all survived, and the show did pretty well, too.

And although I would love to say I was dripping in diamonds and renting baby elephants for birthday parties, with four kids and a job, I just wanted to go one day without leaking breast milk through my shirt (Ray Romano was hoping for the same thing).

I've had quite a ride, and I wouldn't change a second of it. It's been at times thrilling, hilarious, terrifying, and messy, but always human. I'm no celebrity guru; I try to keep my recipes, like my life, simple and satisfying. I mean, come on. I'm the humble forty-ninth grandchild of a Catholic Mother of the Year.

Just waiting for the pope to call.

Feeding Family

When we brought our first baby home from the hospital, I had a mini-freakout: *What do I do?* And it wasn't a rhetorical question, or a long-term one; I honestly didn't know what to do in the next minute, let alone the next hour. And I had no mom to call. *Should I put him down?* I thought. *Do I carry him around?* I paced around the living room, pleading with a drooling newborn for the answers. *When do I go to the bathroom?*

I was *that* clueless. And yet, like just about every other mother in human history, I figured it out. I learned as I went along.

If you're a parent, I trust that you, too, have put together the basic dos and don'ts: Keep 'em warm, dry, and away from electrical sockets, and shove some kind of food in them every time they cry. Those things, along with a generous supply of love, just about cover the basics; no need to get too fancy.

So even though I'm known for playing moms on TV, I'm not here to shout parenting tips from some celebrity mountaintop. Sure, Dave and I had all the baby books to read, but as you probably know, the minute you have a little spare time, all you want to do is pour yourself a glass of wine and zone out to *Wheel of Fortune* . . . maybe that'll be the title

of my parenting book: *Cabernet and Cable: Surviving the Blur of Baby's First Year*!

As the kids got a little older, I continued to shy away from anything fancy, because let's face it, the palate of the average four-year-old is not exactly sophisticated. In fact, at one point we were remodeling our kitchen, and all I had was a microwave and a single portable burner, and it didn't change what I was making for the boys all that much. So yeah, there was a period when we were having hot dogs, spaghetti, and sauce from the jar. Sue me.

But as time went on, I became more inventive and really started to enjoy cooking. Even the simplest things, like slicing the green top off a big, aromatic strawberry, can make for pleasurable moments. The word *mindful* is thrown around a lot lately, but when we slow down, breathe, and settle into the moment, I think it makes a difference—that's when the love sneaks into the food.

So as my family has grown, I've developed more skills in the kitchen, and my meals have become more delicious. And because growing boys are basically eating machines, I am continually challenged to churn out nourishment while accomplishing two goals: first, it has to be interesting enough to keep them happy; and second, simple enough to be repeated without too much fuss.

Wait. I hear the pope at the door . . .

Every once in a while, I invent something pretty neat, if I do say so myself, and this book contains many of my family's delicious mainstays plus a bunch of my experiments in fanciness, like Mascarpone and Raspberry–Stuffed French Toast (page 59) and a Chocolate Chile Tart (page 166). I hope they help to expand your current repertoire.

Finally, cooking for my family has given me a profound appreciation for my own mom. These days, I have lots of modern cooking gadgets, literally millions of recipes (and instructional videos) just a keystroke away, and three organic markets within spitting distance of my house. Meanwhile, my poor mother pulled—no joke—a red wagon to the grocery store once a week by herself. Forget a cell phone, the woman didn't even have a *car*! So looking back, her weekly rotation of simple meals was quite a feat—not to mention a labor of love—and my memories of them only get sweeter with time.

So here are my suggestions for nourishing a growing family.

Have a Routine

Cooking for a family is a nonstop challenge. Unlike parties, which take place only once in a while, family dinners happen every day, all year long. That can be daunting, not to mention a grind.

So as much as I didn't appreciate my mother's meal rotation when I was growing up, I see the practical wisdom in it now. She had her dishes, and they kept her sane, and even if we were bored sometimes, it didn't *kill* us. Kids could use a little boredom these days!

The nice thing about having a weekly or biweekly rotation is that you will get better and better at these dishes, and you will naturally improve upon them, tweaking them creatively: Naked hamburgers one week can be topped with avocado, Cheddar, and sprouts the next; roasted chicken can be made with orange this Sunday, garlic the next, and paprika and thyme after that.

I trust this process, deeply. As an actress, I learn my lines well—repeating them like crazy—so I can become creative with them, trying new ways to say them with varying intentions and attitudes. If I don't get my lines down pat, I can't really play. Without a solid structure, I can't be creative. So it is with cooking.

Finally, as you get more comfortable with a dish, you will relax and put more love into the food. That's real.

Try New Things

I know. I just spent five whole paragraphs telling you to develop a routine. And I meant it. But at the same time, I want to encourage you to try a new recipe—something completely out of your wheelhouse—every once in a while. For some people, that means once a week; for others, once a month. If you tend to forget, put a reminder in your phone about it.

By trying something completely new, you'll be introducing novel ingredients, cooking styles, and taste combinations into your home. This will fire your imagination in the kitchen and give everyone a little break from the routine. Maybe the new recipe will get integrated into the schedule . . . and maybe not. But it will be fun and a change.

When it comes to trying new recipes, I tend to start with desserts. Who doesn't like a sweet thing to eat? I find I'm excited about trying them, and even if the results aren't perfect, no one cares as the whipped cream and custard slide down into their bellies. Sweet is sweet.

So kick yourself out of your routine a little, and everyone will stay energized and happy.

Eat Together

The only thing that Dave and I have been pretty adamant about is eating all together

FIND YOUR LEVEL OF ORGANIZATION

In the next chapter you'll see where my organization gene gets expressed: parties! But when it comes to cooking for a family day in and day out, I don't have specific organizational tips to share. Sure, I've made heroic plans to order everything I needed two weeks ahead, have the perfectly stocked pantry, and chart the cooking plan on a whiteboard like a NASA technician . . . but

after a few days I get distracted; life gets in the way, a kid gets sick, and I just make do with what's in the pantry, the fridge, and the store down the street. I generally have most of what I need for my weekly routine, but that's a groove I've gotten into over time, and you will develop your own. Your family is unique and I trust that you will find the organization level that works for you.

as a family. By the time the boys could handle sitting up in a chair (or even a high chair), we had dinners together almost every night.

Strangely, starring on a hit TV show didn't interfere with this. Because *Everybody Loves Raymond* was what they call a "multi-camera" sitcom, we would rehearse the show like a mini-play during the week, and then shoot it on multiple cameras, in front of a live audience, on Friday night. This meant that my schedule was completely

predictable, and I was able to make it home for dinner almost every night of the week.

Of course, that doesn't mean that every dinner was fun or sprinkled with magical Perfect Family dust, but coming together regularly (with technology turned *off*) is a powerful thing; it's about having a clan, and getting a chance to be seen and heard as a member of that clan. And when the whole clan eats the same food, a deep bonding takes place. I believe that through the breaking of bread, we humans get closer, on a soul level, no matter our religion.

"Oh, thank you, Your Holiness, I really don't deserve this . . ."

So I encourage you to do this sitting-down-as-a-family thing while you can. In my experience, it breaks down at around age fourteen, when your kid doesn't want to talk to you anymore and has too many afterschool activities to make dinner a priority. So the sweet spot is from ages three to fourteen, and if you can hit it, it'll set up your kids for life: Laughter, good conversation, and collective problem-solving are vital to expanding minds, while setting the table, saying grace, and cleaning up after the meal help children form good habits. Finally, every part of the dinner ritual affirms the messages of self-care, community, and respect for other people. How great is that? Who *cares* if they eat Pop-Tarts sometimes!

Kids don't generally say it, but a family-dinner tradition imprints on them. I remember my youngest son had to do an interview where he was asked about our family life and one of his answers surprised me. He said: "Dinner's not as fun now that Sam's not here." You see, his eldest brother had gone off to college, so our clan had been . . . rearranged, you might say. And he felt it. His observation made me realize how important it was that we were sitting down together, really *being* together, as a family unit.

These days, all the boys are over fourteen and have very busy lives. Plus, I now work on *The Middle*, which has a different schedule than *Raymond* did, so cooking for everyone is trickier during shooting season. Our nightly dinner ritual has transformed itself into a weekly Sunday-afternoon feast, in the British tradition. Gathered around a big roasted chicken served with crispy fingerling potatoes, we laugh, and argue, and try to decipher the meaning of obscure Steely Dan lyrics . . . while silently renewing that sacred family bond.

Wow. This medal is *heavy*.

Feeding Friends

There are a million ways to party.

I once attended a soiree thrown by a famous comedian who lived in a big mansion, complete with uniformed butlers. We mingled in a beautiful salon for cocktails, then the butlers ushered us into the dining room for the meal, and finally, we were led outside into the garden for cognac and cigars. It was an extremely fancy, once-in-a-lifetime-unless-you're-Kate-Middleton event, and I had never experienced anything like it.

On the other end of the spectrum, I recently went to a birthday party for a musician friend, and the decor consisted of guitars and microphones, while the "dinner" was a few bags of chips tossed onto a folding card table.

In both cases, everyone had a blast because, as I learned in New York in my twenties, parties are about bringing people together. So the food, the music, the silverware, and all the niggly details, are secondary to the human factor.

Which doesn't mean that making your choices can't be fun and lead to beautiful, delicious results—parties are a form of creative generosity—but it's the guests who make the party.

Especially when you ply them with booze.

So relax. Your party is just another excuse to love the people in your life. No one actually *cares* if the canapés are perfect, or if the wine is a 1964 Château Margaux. Whether they are conscious of it or not, your guests just want to relax, be themselves, and enjoy the warmth of other human beings.

So if you're a stuff-your-brother's-friends-in-the-bathroom hostess, just pour yourself a drink and thumb through the recipes in this book to find something fab for your shindig. Try Watermelon and Feta Kabobs (page 74) and A Glorious Cheese Board (page 79)—they're easy and delicious.

If, however, you've got some time before your party and don't mind doing some planning, this chapter is for you. In it, I cover all the things you need to consider in order to throw a well-prepared bash. And by diving into the little details, you'll ultimately be freed up to enjoy your fantastic party. I've peppered the practical suggestions with some party anecdotes, observations, and other tips to keep you a happy, organized social butterfly.

Patty's Party Planning Prescription

First, get a pen and paper . . . yes, I recommend going old school on this one, although it's not required. Planning a party is all about making comprehensive lists of what needs to be done and then getting the sweet, sweet satisfaction of checking everything off them.

This method is simple, and I've broken it down into the five questions used by reporters, like my dad, when getting to the

GETTING ORGANIZED

Organization didn't exactly come naturally to me; as an *artiste*, I was more the clothes-thrown-all-over-the-floor type until I became friends with a restaurant consultant in New York City. Now, this guy was *organized*: His shirts were neatly pressed and hung like soldiers in his closet; his kitchen was immaculate; and don't get me started on his bathroom!

One day, I was having a bit of an actress-y fit about everything I had to get done, how *hard* my life was, and that I could never possibly handle the stress of it all. Instead of launching sweaters and underwear, I was tossing articles of emotional clothing all over his floor. After indulging my one-woman production of *Who's Afraid of Virginia Woolf?* for a while, he'd had enough. Calmly, and with real composure, he pulled out a gold pen and his little leather notebook, and looked me in the eye:

"Okay, what are the three things you have to do?"

This stopped me in my tracks. I was being asked to cease emoting and to start thinking. I had to prioritize. There was silence for a beat, while I reeled my energy back into my brain.

"Uh . . . prepare for my audition . . ."
He wrote it down.
"Send my rent check . . ."
"Yes?"
"And sell my plasma to pay for my therapist!"

He cocked his head and thought for a second.

"I'll cover that, Patty."

Mr. Restaurant made his final scribble and returned the top to his pen. He carefully ripped out the page he'd written on and handed it to me.

"Here," he said. "Now you know where to start."

Of course, there were more than three things on my entire to-do list, but those first ones were the most important, and therefore carried the most charge. Seeing them, just three neat lines on a piece of paper, cut my stress level by half.

These days, I carry a notebook around everywhere, and with so much going on, I couldn't live without it. So when the stress starts to build (and it does), I can translate it all into neat lines on a page, and my blood pressure comes right down. It works every time!

meat of a story. They are known as the Five W's:

1. Why?
2. Who?
3. When?
4. Where?
5. What?

By asking each of these questions, we cover every conceivable angle of your next bash.

Let's take a look:

Why?

The first question to ask yourself is why you're having a party. Is there a specific occasion? If so, write it down. Party intentions may include:

- To celebrate a person, a holiday, or an accomplishment
- To catch up with old friends
- To introduce new friends
- To play games
- To dance and blow off steam
- To raise money for a charity

This may seem like a simple question, but getting clear about the party's intention can bring clarity to all your other decisions. For instance, I recently threw a birthday dinner for Dave. The intention was: to celebrate my husband! By writing down that simple intention, it sort of organized all my actions around it.

I'll give you an example: Dave loves pomegranates, so I made sure there was a special pomegranate drink for everyone

MIXING IT UP

Dave and I have been blessed with many friends from all walks of life, and I regularly invite guests to our home who are on opposite ends of the political spectrum. You see, when it comes to party conversation, I'm that weirdo who goes straight for the taboo subjects like religion and politics. Although exchanges can be slightly nerve-wracking at moments, I find them to be part of what makes a good party. In my opinion, as long as we have the foundation of love and respect, we should be able to challenge one another on our beliefs and suppositions while remaining kind.

But that's just me.

You're planning *your* party, and it's important that you bring together the mix of individuals that feels right to you. Don't aim for perfection—humans will always confound you—but perhaps surprising your aunt Jean with the guy who jilted her at the altar thirty years ago will make for a little *too* much drama.

You decide. What group of people feels good to you?

GUEST GOODIES

I loved birthday parties when I was a kid, and the best part—beyond the cake and the ice cream—was the bag of party favors given out at the door. I loved the feeling of digging into my grab bag to find candy or a toy or a piece of gaudy plastic jewelry. So these days, if I'm not too busy, I often make little gifts for my guests to take home with them. That way, the party goes out the door with the guest, and the celebratory vibe lasts a few more days. You'll see guest goodies mentioned later in this section, and there's a whole section of recipes for them starting on page 207. Enjoy!

at the bar, and pomegranate seeds in the salad . . . little stuff like that. Now, I'm not saying I wouldn't have thought of those things anyway, but by writing down my overall intention, I kept my heart, and mind, continually coming back to celebrating Dave.

Even while he was crunching pretzels—loudly—over my shoulder.

Figuring out your intention also helps to crank up your imagination about the decor, music, activities, and food choices . . . but I'm getting ahead of myself.

Next question . . .

Who?

What group of lucky souls are you inviting to this blowout?

- How many people are you inviting? The number of people will help you to determine other things, like whether it's a sit-down dinner, buffet, or cocktail party.
- How are you going to invite them? Through email, text, phone call, or old-fashioned written invitation?

- Do any of the guests have special needs?
- Do any of the guests follow special diets?

By thinking this through, you can avoid hurt feelings, social mishaps, and accidentally killing the guests who have nut allergies.

When?

This is an obvious but very important question: When is this Party-to-End-All-Parties taking place?

Now's the time to look at some dates and make sure the major players (husband, kids, guests of honor) don't have conflicts that day. If you plan to hire helpers for the party, you need to make sure they're available, too.

Where?

This question brings up all kinds of physical issues, like:

- Are you throwing this bash at home or do you need to find a venue?
- If you need a venue, what's your budget?

ACTS OF GOD

Dave and I threw a party the night of the big Northridge earthquake in 1994. It was a lovely January night, and our first son, Sam, was almost one. I remember I had made a ginger pasta dish for dinner (I got the recipe from a friend and it was absolutely *scrumptious*).

Most of our guests were friends of Dave's from England, so they were staying overnight, and I'm pretty sure they weren't expecting the little treat Mother Nature had in store for us . . .

At 4:30 a.m., I was half-asleep, nursing Sam, when the whole house began to shake. We lived just twenty miles from Northridge, and the quake, which registered 6.7 on the Richter scale, lasted about twenty seconds—a looooooong time when the earth is rolling, your house starts jerking back and forth, and there's a baby to protect.

It felt like forever.

After it passed, our whole block poured out onto the street to check the damage, and I remember noticing that my neighbors, also awoken in the middle of the night, had put on bathrobes . . . but they weren't normal bathrobes; this being L.A., the robes had the logos of various TV shows stitched on them because most of our neighbors were in the business! In post-earthquake shock, all I could think was: "You work on *Seinfeld*?"

That was a party I'll never forget.

- If at home, where exactly in your home? Is the party a moving affair or a sit-down event?
- How do you envision the flow of the party?
- Will it be indoor/outdoor? Is weather a factor?
- Do you have enough space for all these people?
- Do you need to rent some furniture to accommodate these guests, or pull some up from the basement?
- What's the parking situation at your home? Will there be ample room for all your guests to park nearby?
- Where are they going to put their coats or gifts they might bring?
- What is the atmosphere you'd like to achieve?
- How do you plan to achieve it? (Lighting? Music? Centerpieces? Costumes? Your outfit?)
- Who's in charge of setting up and cleaning up? Do you need help?

Okay, so I've covered a lot of territory here with the "where?" question. But it's important to think through the physical reality of throwing a party. For instance, guests will need to use a restroom, so which one is it? And who's going to make sure it's clean before they arrive—with hand towels and enough toilet paper?

SETTING THE MOOD

TUNES

When it comes to music, Dave and I are suckers for stuff from the 1940s. And it's perfect party music—jazzy and sophisticated but fun. Whether it's Frank, or Ella, or one of the big bands, putting on '40s music tends to set an upbeat, happy mood.

My other party go-to is anything Motown. You name the artist: Smokey Robinson; the Supremes: Stevie Wonder . . . the rich sounds of Motown music tend to keep guests energized yet relaxed. It's the very best music for romance, too.

But you knew that.

Party mix don'ts? For me, it's any music that is dissonant or angry. You may love screaming along with Rage Against the Machine in the car, but when you're bringing together humans, choose sounds that help them relax and feel united.

Back in the day I would haul out all my albums and make mix tapes, but again, technology has come to the rescue with services like Pandora and Spotify, which are just amazing. Party mix at your fingertips!

DECOR

I *looooove* a good candle. Not only is candlelight naturally beautiful, enough of it can really shift the feeling of a room. If you have dimmer switches on your lights and can adjust the mood of your party space, great, but if not, you may want to depend on just a few select lamps and lean heavily on candles. Placed (safely) on mantels, side tables, coffee tables, and bookshelves—not to mention the dining room table—candles will bring a certain magic to your party. Just be sure to keep any scented candles away from the food and dining area, as they can really mix up the senses and interfere with your meal. If you love scented candles, reserve them for the entrance and the bathroom.

Fresh flowers are also natural energy-lifters. These days, most big grocery stores have floral sections; one big bouquet can be divided into three or four lovely mini-arrangements that will spread the joy around. Arranged artfully, flowers never fail to please.

By asking yourself to consider these questions, you'll face fewer stressful surprises on the day.

What?

This is the nitty-gritty, my friend. It's where things get real: lists are written, checked, double-checked, and eventually checked off. And that feels fantastic. The more you think everything through, the more serene your preparation time will be—and the more fun you'll have at your own party. I promise.

So get your pen or pencil ready . . . The first question is:

What are you going to serve?

Depending on the party, this could be simple or complicated. Let's break it down into categories:

Appetizers
Main course
Dessert
Liquor
Other beverages
Guest goodies (see page 207)

Write them all down. If you're not sure yet about a certain category, do some recipe searching or simply sleep on it. Either way, begin to develop your menu and bar choices.

Now we start making our lists. When I'm planning I draw up five separate lists, each on its own piece of paper.

1. *Groceries:* What exact ingredients are needed for each dish? If you need to cook multiple batches of certain recipes, now's the time to do the math and figure out amounts. This may be a little tedious, but getting this work done now eliminates possible last-minute panics. A comprehensive shopping list is a beautiful thing, and when I really want to be a detail nerd, I organize my list into sections—veggies, meat, and so on—so I can cruise the grocery store more efficiently.

P.S. Alcohol and bar ingredients fall into this category, too. Don't forget ice!

2. *Cookware:* What exact tools do you need to make each dish? Do you have enough baking sheets? The mixer for the cupcake batter? Oven space? Figure it out and write down all the tools and appliances required to make the meal. It's a good idea to consult recipes carefully at this point to avoid that *I forgot to get the freakin' cupcake liners!* feeling.

BAR TIPS

Unless you met all your friends at an AA meeting, there's probably going to be alcohol flowing at your party. Here are a few tips to make your bar more manageable.

- **LIMIT THE CHOICES:** Serve just one white wine and one red. There's no need to have an endless variety of wine for a party, but it is important that you have enough; better to overbuy than to run dry.

- **IF YOU SERVE SPIRITS, GET THE MAJORS:** vodka, gin, and whiskey. Between those and some mixers, you've covered all the bases.

- **CONSIDER MAKING A SPECIALTY COCKTAIL:** This can be fun, creative, and keep the choices simple for your guests. Take a look at the delicious cocktail and punch recipes later in this book, or think up your own unique drink that's related to the party's theme. We have a margarita machine that we haul out at least once every summer. It's fun!

CALIFORNIA CASUAL

Los Angeles is simply not a formal place. Sure, I own some nice outfits because I've had the good fortune to be invited to some award shows, but off the red carpet, there's really nowhere to wear them.

California casual, however, should never be confused with California *cheap*. I was invited to a lovely Malibu birthday party recently, and it seems that getting dressed up—Malibu style—is putting on an eight-hundred-dollar pair of jeans, a cashmere cable knit sweater (casually drooping off one shoulder), and a big, gold cuff bracelet. That's the uniform. Technically, you're casual because you're wearing jeans, but the whole ensemble could pay off my mortgage! Oh, California . . .

3. *Servingware:* How are you going to serve these drinks and dishes? Do you have enough serving bowls, platters, plates, utensils, napkins, placemats, and glasses for all your guests? Do you need more? Or are you going casual, using paper plates and napkins around the barbecue? Think it through carefully. Write down what you need and what you may need to buy, rent, or borrow.

4. *Atmosphere:* What needs to happen to the space? Cleaning? Decorating? Do you need to purchase some items for the decor? Move some furniture? What music do you plan to play? Considering all these details will help stir your creativity and get you thinking about your party atmosphere. This should also be where you consider what you want to wear, or try to force your teenage sons to wear (good luck with that).

5. *Help:* Do you need your kids or partner to pitch in? Will you need a babysitter that night? Would you like help from someone to pass around the appetizers? Do you need to hire your neighbor's kid to help with the cooking? Rent any equipment or furniture? Don't be afraid to pay your more responsible kids—or your neighbor's kids—to be waiters or waitresses for a few hours. It's well worth it.

So, those are your lists. Between them, you should see just about everything you need to do and buy or acquire before your party. Although it may seem overwhelming at first, by making these lists roughly seven to ten days before your party, you'll be able to plot a serene and happy path to your fiesta.

Finally, I organize the tasks into doable chunks and give myself one or two jobs pertaining to the party every day for the week leading up to the big event. It might look like this:

Friday (1 week before the party): Send Dave to buy booze.

Call around to hire a helper, if needed—a friend's teenage kid or a neighborhood college student—to assist with cooking and serving at the party.

Saturday: Pull out all the servingware and leave it on the dining room table. Make sure I have everything I need.

Sunday: Execute my initial atmosphere decisions (move furniture, buy candles and other decor items, and organize music). Get kids to pull chairs out from basement.

Monday: Buy the groceries and any servingware items I need.

Tuesday: Set the table. (Yes, I have been known to set the table as early as Tuesday. Who cares? I don't have to think about it again, and looking at the pretty table makes me excited for the party.)

Wednesday: Set up the bar (minus the ice). Organize what I'll wear.

Thursday: Prep cook (with hired helper, if necessary). Cook anything that can be done beforehand.

Friday: Final cooking with helper. Do final atmosphere tweaks (put out ice, light candles, arrange flowers). Get dressed, press play on the iPad, and . . . *party*!

Phew. By getting the little details handled early, you can stop worrying and open your heart to your loved ones. Preparing for the party becomes so relaxed that it's like a massage for you, so by the time you get to the party, cocktail in hand, you feel—and look—fantastic.

So, now that we've discussed feeding family, and friends, it's time to get into the kitchen. We start with kitchen setup. After that, you'll find a hundred of my favorite recipes, from fancy appetizers to serious comfort food. I'm so very happy to share them with you. . . . Let's go!

STAYING ON TRACK

I'm constantly amazed by technology these days. Not only can I look up a recipe on my phone—in the middle of cooking a meal—if I'm really in a pinch, I can press a button and have a forgotten item delivered straight to my door! It's a whole new world.

But mostly I use my phone as a backup brain. With the "Reminder" function, or through the Calendar app, I give myself little digital pokes and prods to get things done. So I encourage you to take photos of all your lists (no more losing bits of paper!), and to schedule your tasks into your phone, in case you're prone to forgetting.

Wait. Where's my phone?

Kitchen Setup

Chances are you already have some great tools in your kitchen. It doesn't take much to be able to make delicious dishes, so let's not get crazy about having the perfect setup before diving in. Here are my basic tools—the ones that make my cooking possible day in and day out:

- Blender
- Cutting board
- Food processor
- Good pots and pans (I like Calphalon)
- Good whisk
- Hand mixer
- Knife sharpener
- Measuring cups and spoons
- Really good knives (I like Henkel)
- Spatulas
- Strainers
- Wooden spoons

Here are other things that I've collected over the years that I use very often (and all of them are used at least once in the recipes that follow):

Appliances
- Pancake griddle
- Waffle iron

Tools
- Deep-fry thermometer
- Instant-read cooking thermometer
- Kitchen scissors
- Potato masher
- Scoops (various sizes)
- Skewers
- Slotted spoons

Baking needs
- Baking pans (various sizes)
- Baking sheets
- Cookie cutters
- Muffin tins
- Pastry bag
- Pie plates
- Rolling pin
- Wire rack

Wrapping, storing, miscellaneous
- Paper towels
- Parchment paper
- Plastic wrap
- Tea towels
- Wax paper
- Zip-top bags

- Ice pop molds
- Jars for pickling and jams
- Mason jars

But don't let this list overwhelm you. I tend to buy kitchen tools as I need them. For instance, when I first read a recipe that made veggie "noodles," I went out and got a spiralizer. It wasn't expensive, and I found it in the kitchenware section of my grocery store, along with—to my surprise—graters, zesters, meat tenderizers, and any number of other cool kitchen gadgets. Turns out you don't need to pitch a tent at Williams-Sonoma to have a fancy kitchen!

If you're not sure you'll need a specific tool for the long run, don't be afraid to borrow it from a sibling or friend. For instance, you may not need to own a waffle maker if you're only going to do them twice a year. You can also find fantastic—often vintage—tools and appliances at yard sales or online.

So unless you're the kind of person who needs the perfect kitchen *today*, I encourage you to build your kitchen over time. Because I've been cooking for many years, I now own lots of things, but I acquired each item as I needed it, for a particular dish or occasion. So now my kitchen is more like a little museum of feeding my loved ones. I like that.

My Bare-Bones Pantry

Okay, these are things I have on hand *all the time*; they are the bare bones of my pantry, and by adding meat and vegetables to this handful of ingredients, I can make any number of delicious dishes.

- Bread crumbs
- Extra virgin olive oil
- Flour
- Garlic (every dish is better with grilled onions and garlic)
- Herbs and spices
- Lemons
- Noodles/pasta
- Onions
- Pepper (in a good pepper grinder)
- Sea salt (in a good salt grinder)
- Sugar
- Tomatoes
- Vodka (It really helps to have a drink when you're cooking. It makes the experience much more pleasant!)
- Limes (for the vodka)

In the refrigerator
- Butter
- Chicken. I always have chicken in the fridge.
- Eggs
- Parmesan cheese
- Pesto. I love pesto.

But that's me. And this book is for you and your family and friends. Because you are the one who knows—and loves—them, you know what they need.

So, before we move on to the recipes, I have one more little story:

I was very ambitious when I first started having kids. After weaning my second baby, I

decided that a smart thing to do was to hire someone to give me piano lessons! Sure, I had a one- and two-year-old running around the house, but I wasn't going to let that stop me.

Well, I managed only five lessons, but I noticed something during that time. After my last forty-five-minute session, during which I had focused so completely on the piano, I felt like I'd had a great massage. Or that I'd been lying on a warm beach . . .

I felt *cleansed*.

And I realized I wanted that *feeling* more than I wanted to be the next Chopin.

Believe it or not, our minds like to focus. On a single task. The world may seem chaotic, but the human mind likes to settle, even dig in a little. And I experience that when working in the kitchen—it's become a meditative practice, and a way to disengage from all the noise. And at the end of my efforts, I have a lovely dish to nourish myself, my family, and my wonderful friends.

It's a win-win-win.

Let's cook . . .

Before We Begin

As far as I'm concerned, anytime you want to take a shortcut, go ahead.

Need to buy premade dough for a pie? Do it.

Want to buy a bottle of cherry juice instead of making your own? Go for it.

Cooking is not like running a marathon, where taking the subway for the last mile is cheating. No one's looking. So unless the recipe specifies otherwise, feel free to take the subway.

Shortcuts are fine.

part two

Recipes

Breakfast: Everyday Eats and Weekend Wonders

They say that breakfast is the most important meal of the day, but they never mention that it can be the most delicious, too. Our household is very busy in the morning, so I try to have things ready for on-the-go breakfasts, like muffins and scones, but on the weekends, we can relax and indulge in an elegant brunch: think stuffed waffles or spinach and cheese strata with a side of candied bacon. You'll find all sorts of great ideas and mouthwatering recipes for your morning rituals in this section.

MAKE IT FANCY

This is a very versatile recipe, and you can use just about any berry you like. But don't stop there: I love to add minced fresh herbs (about 1 teaspoon) like rosemary or thyme to the dry ingredients, before adding liquids. You can also try adding about ⅓ cup chopped nuts, such as pistachios or almonds, for a bit of crunch. Explore. Mix and match. You've got the rest of your life to develop your perfect "scahn"!

World's Best Waffles

I love making waffles, because the waffles *are* the presentation; they're just cool! In this recipe, I incorporate sour cream, which gives the waffles a certain richness and subtle zing. Plus, the waffle is a fantastic delivery system for other foods both sweet and savory. I've included a recipe here for Fried Chicken Bites (page 40) to be served on waffles, but you can create a sweet waffle bar, with diced fruit, compotes, syrups, whipped cream, and ice cream. With four kids, a waffle bar makes everyone happy.

Makes six 7-inch Belgian-style waffles

2 cups all-purpose flour
1 tablespoon baking powder
1 tablespoon sugar
½ teaspoon sea salt
1 cup 2% or whole milk
¾ cup sour cream

2 large eggs, lightly beaten
1 teaspoon pure vanilla extract
6 tablespoons (¾ stick) unsalted
   butter, melted
Cooking spray, optional
Pure maple syrup, to serve

1. In a medium bowl, whisk together the flour, baking powder, sugar, and salt.
2. Add the milk, sour cream, eggs, and vanilla to the bowl. Stir with a fork until just combined. Stir in the butter and let the batter rest for 5 minutes.
3. Meanwhile, heat a waffle iron according to manufacturer instructions.
4. Spray the waffle iron with cooking spray, if needed. Ladle enough batter to cover two thirds of the surface (the rest will spread once you close the top). The waffle is cooked through when you see all the steam has stopped shooting out the sides of the iron. Repeat with the remaining batter
5. Serve the waffles hot with syrup as they are ready. If you'd like to serve them all at once, you can keep them warm, on a platter, in a 250°F oven.

Fried Chicken Bites (for Waffles)

Makes 6 servings

1½ pounds boneless chicken breasts,
  cut into strips or chunks
¾ cup buttermilk
1¾ cups all-purpose flour
1½ teaspoons garlic powder

¾ teaspoon smoked paprika
¾ teaspoon fine sea salt
Freshly ground black pepper
3 large egg whites, lightly beaten
Extra virgin olive oil

1. Combine the chicken and buttermilk in a medium bowl.
2. In a small bowl, combine the flour, garlic powder, paprika, salt, and pepper. Whisk to blend.
3. Remove a piece of chicken from the buttermilk, letting any excess drip off. Dip it into the flour mixture, shaking off any excess flour. Dip into the egg white, then into the flour mixture again, shaking off any excess. Transfer the chicken to a plate and repeat with the remaining pieces of chicken. Let sit for 10 minutes.
4. Meanwhile, adjust an oven rack to the upper-middle position and place an 11 × 17-inch rimmed baking sheet on the rack. Preheat the oven to 450°F.
5. When the oven reaches 450°F, remove the baking sheet. Swirl on enough oil to coat the bottom of the tray. Place the pieces of chicken on the tray (they'll sizzle once they touch the hot oil). Bake, turning once, for 25 minutes, or until golden and crisp on both sides.

Best Pancakes in the World

We love pancakes in our household. I make them, my boys make them, and there have even been occasions when pancakes have been served for dinner. But there is a slight division in our ranks; my sons like chocolate chips, while Dave is a blueberry man. . . . So we signed a truce, in pancake batter, and combined them in this recipe. It's delicious.

And a heads-up: I'm not a fan of huge pancakes like you'd get at a pancake house; I find them harder to cook and harder to flip, and they often leave leftovers (which get thrown out). These are about four inches across, but make what works for you.

Makes eight 4-inch pancakes

1 cup all-purpose flour
2 teaspoons baking powder
1 teaspoon sugar
½ teaspoon baking soda
¼ teaspoon sea salt
1 large egg
1¼ to 1½ cups buttermilk

1 tablespoon unsalted butter, melted, plus more to coat the skillet
½ teaspoon pure vanilla extract
¼ cup mini chocolate chips
½ cup frozen wild blueberries (such as Wyman's)
Pure maple syrup or confectioners' sugar, to serve

1. In a medium bowl, whisk together the flour, baking powder, sugar, baking soda, and salt.
2. Add the egg, 1¼ cups buttermilk (more if you prefer thinner pancakes), melted butter, and vanilla. Stir just until the batter is combined and there are no visible signs of flour.
3. Fold in the chocolate chips and frozen blueberries. Let the batter rest for 5 minutes.
4. Meanwhile, melt a pat of butter in a medium or large skillet over medium-low heat. Drop ¼ cup of batter into the skillet. Cook until the edges begin to dry and little bubbles form on top. Flip and cook 1 to 2 minutes more, until done to your liking. Serve hot with maple syrup or confectioners' sugar.

ARE YOU READY?

To test if the skillet is properly heated, sprinkle a few drops of water on it. They should "dance" across the surface.

Blueberry Maple Pecan Overnight Oats

The verdict is in, and oats are really, really good for you. High in fiber, they help to keep everything moving while lowering your cholesterol and tasting creamy and delicious. This recipe also contains chia seeds, another superfood that's high in protein and omega-3 fatty acids. But the best part of this recipe is how easy it is . . . add milk at night and voilà, a creamy oat delight—with a tapioca-esque twist—for breakfast on the way to work! I love that.

Makes 4 servings

SPECIAL EQUIPMENT
4 pint-size glass mason jars with lids

1 cup old-fashioned oats (not quick cooking)
¼ cup chia seeds
4 teaspoons pure maple syrup

¼ cup dried blueberries
Ground cinnamon
2 cups 2% or whole milk (or your preferred dairy-free substitute)
¼ cup toasted pecans, chopped (see "Toasting Nuts," opposite)

1. In each of the mason jars, combine ¼ cup oats, 1 tablespoon chia seeds, 1 teaspoon syrup, 1 tablespoon blueberries, and a pinch of cinnamon. Add ½ cup of milk to each jar.
2. Secure the lids tightly and shake the jars to mix the contents. Place in the fridge overnight.
3. When ready to serve, sprinkle 1 tablespoon of chopped pecans on top of each.

TOASTING NUTS

There are two methods:

1. **IN A SKILLET:** Place the nuts in a skillet over medium to medium-low heat. Give the pan a shake every minute or so, as nuts can burn quickly (and the oilier the nut, the more easily it can burn). Cooking times vary from 4 to 7 minutes depending on the variety of nut. They are ready when they give off a fragrant smell and are lightly golden.

2. **IN THE OVEN:** Spread the nuts in a single layer on a baking sheet and toast them at 350ºF until they begin to smell fragrant, 8 to 10 minutes.

BURN NOTICE: If you lose track and the nuts burn (it happens to the best of us), it's better to discard them all and start again. Burned nuts cannot be un-burned, and the acrid taste will ruin an entire recipe. Aw, nuts!

Spicy Baked Avocado Eggs

Both avocados and eggs will give you long-lasting, slow-burning fuel for the day. By adding cotija, red pepper flakes, and chorizo, you'll get a spicy kick on your way out the door. I like this dish not only for its flavors, but because it's a nice break from carbs at breakfast.

Makes 4 servings

4 eggs
2 tablespoons crumbled cotija cheese
Splash of heavy cream
Sea salt
Crushed red pepper flakes

Freshly ground black pepper
2 avocados
¼ cup cooked crumbled chorizo
   or salsa

1. Preheat the oven to 425°F.
2. In a medium bowl, combine the eggs, cotija, cream, salt, red pepper flakes, and pepper in a medium bowl. Beat with a fork until well mixed.
3. Halve and pit the avocados (do not peel them). Depending on the size of the avocado pits, you might need to use a spoon to shave a little bit of extra avocado from the center to accommodate the egg filling.
4. Arrange the avocados cut side up in a small, rimmed baking dish (they should be snug enough to not roll around). Carefully pour egg filling into the center of each avocado (do not overfill).
5. Bake 12 to 15 minutes, until the filling is lightly golden on top.
6. Spoon 1 tablespoon chorizo or salsa on top of each avocado half. Serve hot.

Candied Bacon

When you have the time to do something special, or are having friends over for brunch, try this recipe. It's fantastic. Because the bacon can burn easily at the end of the cooking, be sure to start checking it at twenty minutes to prevent a porky disaster.

Makes 4 servings

8 ounces bacon
¼ cup packed light brown sugar

1. Preheat the oven to 350°F. Line an 11 × 17-inch rimmed baking sheet with a piece of parchment paper long enough to hang slightly over the sides.
2. Combine the bacon and sugar in a large bowl. Toss it together, working the sugar into the bacon with your fingertips. Arrange the bacon slices in a single layer on the prepared pan.
3. Bake 20 to 25 minutes, turning halfway through, until bacon is crisp-looking (it may not seem it when you take it from the oven, but it'll continue to crisp after you take it out). Serve hot.

MAKE IT FANCY

Espresso Candied Bacon: Combine 1 teaspoon instant espresso granules with the bacon and sugar.

Sweet and Spicy Candied Bacon: Combine 2 to 3 teaspoons habanero hot sauce with the bacon and sugar.

Apple and Cheese Danish

Fun Fact #1: The Danish isn't really Danish, as it was brought to Denmark by Austrian bakers who crossed the picket lines of striking Danish bakers. So it's actually an Austrian labor-busting pastry, adapted by the Danes. Who knew?

Fun Fact #2: Danishes rock. By combining cheese, fruit, and puff pastry, those Austrians created something very special, enjoyed in diners and coffee shops the world over.

This recipe makes two Danishes. You can bake one right away and freeze the second one if you want. Just set the second Danish on a waxed paper–lined pan in the freezer until firm, then wrap it tightly in plastic wrap. Bake it straight from the freezer (without the plastic, of course)—no need to thaw—for an extra 10 minutes. If you're baking one Danish now and the second one later, make only a half batch of the icing at this point. It's best to make another half batch of fresh icing when you bake the second Danish.

Makes 16 servings

2 Granny Smith apples, peeled, cored, and thinly sliced
2 tablespoons granulated sugar
1 tablespoon all-purpose flour, plus more as needed
1 teaspoon ground cinnamon
½ teaspoon ground allspice
Pinch of sea salt
Zest and juice of 1 lemon

One 8-ounce package cream cheese, softened
1 large egg, separated
1¼ cups confectioners' sugar
½ teaspoon pure vanilla extract
2 sheets puff pastry, thawed
1 tablespoon unsalted butter, melted

1. Preheat the oven 400°F. Line an 11 × 17-inch rimmed baking sheet with parchment paper.
2. In a medium bowl, combine the apples, granulated sugar, flour, cinnamon, allspice, salt, and lemon zest and juice. Set aside.
3. In a separate medium bowl, combine the cream cheese, egg yolk, ¼ cup of the confectioners' sugar, and the vanilla. Stir with a fork until well blended. Set aside.
4. Beat the egg white with a splash of water. Set aside.
5. Unfold one sheet of puff pastry onto a lightly floured countertop. Roll the dough into a 10 × 12-inch rectangle. Snip off the two top corners at an angle. Cut two notches at the bottom of the dough (see the photo, page 48). Cut 1-inch diagonal strips on the right third of the dough. Repeat this on the left third of the dough.

6. Spread half of the cream cheese filling down the center of the dough, leaving a 1-inch border at the top and bottom.
7. Spread half of the apple filling over the cream cheese filling.
8. Fold the top and bottom pieces of dough over the filling. Fold the strips of dough in a crisscross pattern to make a mock braid covering the filling. When you get to the last strip, dab a bit of the egg wash underneath to keep it secure. Lightly brush the Danish with the egg wash.
9. Repeat with the remaining sheet of puff pastry, filling, and cream cheese mixture.
10. Place the Danishes on the prepared pan. Bake until the pastry is deep golden brown and the filling is bubbling, about 25 minutes.
11. In a small bowl, combine the remaining 1 cup confectioners' sugar and the butter with 1 tablespoon of water and whisk until smooth. Drizzle the icing over each Danish. Let sit at least 10 minutes before serving, to allow the filling and the icing to set.

Lemon-Glazed Blueberry Doughnuts

As far as I'm concerned, blueberries should be in—or on—just about everything. In this recipe, I've put freeze-dried blueberries (if you can't find them, try your favorite sprinkles) on glazed doughnuts, and I can't tell you how great it feels to serve these to my family or to bring them out as a fun dessert for friends. Doughnuts, fresh out of the oven, will earn you that World's Greatest Mom mug. ***Makes 6 doughnuts***

DOUGHNUTS
Cooking spray
1 scant cup all-purpose flour
¼ cup sugar
1 teaspoon baking powder
¼ teaspoon sea salt
1 large egg
⅓ cup plus 1 tablespoon 2% or
 whole milk
2 tablespoons unsalted butter,
 melted

GLAZE
1 cup confectioners' sugar
1½ tablespoons freshly squeezed
 lemon juice
1 tablespoon unsalted butter,
 melted

Freeze-dried blueberries or other
 desired toppings

1. Preheat the oven to 425F°. Generously coat a 6-doughnut pan with cooking spray.
2. Make the doughnuts: In a medium bowl, combine the flour, sugar, baking powder, and salt. Whisk to blend.
3. Add the egg, milk, and melted butter. Stir until just mixed, with no visible traces of flour.
4. Spoon the batter into the prepared pan. Bake until the doughnuts spring back when tapped, 7 to 8 minutes. Set the tray on a wire rack to cool completely.
5. Make the glaze: Combine the confectioners' sugar, lemon juice, and butter in a small bowl. Whisk until smooth. Dip the top of the doughnuts into the glaze, letting any excess fall back into the bowl. Sprinkle a few blueberries on top and let sit for at least 15 minutes to allow the glaze to set.

Mini Elderberry Jam Doughnuts

I am a huge sucker for British jam doughnuts (called jelly doughnuts here in the United States). In fact, the first thing I do upon touching down on U.K. soil is buy a big bag of jam doughnuts and go to town on them. Here in L.A., where I need to watch my figure for the camera, I have a system worked out. When jam doughnuts show up on the snack table on the set of *The Middle*, Atticus Shaffer (he plays my son Brick) and I will split one, because we are trying to be *healthy*. Of course, this being America, the doughnut is the size of both our heads, but still, we are showing restraint, and are always quite impressed with ourselves.

This recipe makes mini-doughnuts, and even though I think mini-izing anything guarantees you'll end up eating even more, it just feels better.

Makes 8 to 10 mini-doughnuts

SPECIAL EQUIPMENT
Deep-fry thermometer

1 teaspoon active dry yeast
1/3 cup 2% or whole milk, heated to 110°F
1 cup bread flour
1 large egg yolk
1/2 teaspoon pure vanilla extract
2 teaspoons superfine sugar (see "Sweet Confusion," page 54)

Generous pinch of sea salt
1 1/2 tablespoons unsalted butter, softened
Canola or safflower oil, for frying
Granulated or confectioners' sugar, optional
1/2 cup elderberry jam (or any jam you like)

1. In a large bowl, combine the yeast and milk. Stir in half the flour. Using a hand mixer, beat in the egg yolk and vanilla until just blended, 15 to 30 seconds. Add the remaining flour, superfine sugar, and salt and beat until just mixed, about 30 seconds. Add the butter. Beat until the dough is smooth, about 15 seconds.

2. Cover the bowl with a clean towel or plastic wrap, and let sit in a warm, draft-free place until doubled in volume, about 30 minutes. Gently press down the dough, re-cover, and refrigerate for 1 hour.

3. Line a baking sheet with a clean cloth kitchen towel. Place the dough on a lightly floured counter or cutting board and roll it into a 1/2-inch-thick circle. Press out

circles using a 2½-inch round cutter—you should have between 8 and 10 circles if you reroll the scraps once. Place the doughnuts on the prepared baking sheet and cover gently with another cloth towel. Place in a warm, draft-free place until doubled in volume, about 20 minutes.

4. Meanwhile, fill a 4-quart pot with 2 inches of the oil. Heat to 360°F, using a deep-fry thermometer to test the temperature. Line a plate with paper towels. Add 2 or 3 doughnuts at a time and fry for 1 to 2 minutes per side, or until golden. Place on the paper towel–lined dish to drain. Repeat with the remaining doughnuts.

5. While the doughnuts are still slightly warm, roll them in granulated sugar, if desired (if using confectioners' sugar, wait until they are filled to sprinkle it over them).

6. Fit a pastry bag with a wide round tip. Place the jam in the bag. Insert the tip into one side of the doughnut and fill. Repeat with the rest of the doughnuts. These are best served within a few hours of being made.

SWEET CONFUSION

What is superfine sugar? And while we're at it, what the heck is confectioners' sugar?

Time to get our sweets straight!

Superfine sugar is, as it sounds, very fine, and doughnuts require this type of sugar in order to be nice and light. Although it's available in stores, you can also make superfine sugar at home by blending 1 cup plus 2 teaspoons of regular white (granulated) sugar in a blender for 30 seconds. This will give you 1 cup of superfine sugar.

Confectioners' sugar, a.k.a. powdered sugar, a.k.a. icing sugar, includes a tiny bit of cornstarch and goes by so many names you'd think it had committed a felony. Is being delicious illegal?

POACHING THE SUBJECT

Poached eggs can actually be made a day or two in advance. Store them in a covered container, and reheat in a pot of boiling water for 30 to 60 seconds.

Finger Foods and Little Bites

There's nothing like a good appetizer; it gets everyone's juices flowing for the main meal and can offer a nice balance to drinks being served. Whether you're having a standup cocktail party, a holiday meal, or just a Sunday afternoon lounge with some friends, here are great recipes—dips, chips, and even kebabs—for keeping everyone happy.

BBQ Beef Sliders

When I first came across sliders, I thought, *Isn't this just a mini . . . burger?* They made no sense. But now, after having plucked countless sliders off of trays circulating at Hollywood parties, I've figured out that they're three things: First, they're scrumptious. Second, they're vehicles for a variety of delicious toppings, like the coleslaw in this recipe. And third, they're another example of how we have mini-ized food, which makes us feel better about scarfing down six of them during a cocktail party conversation!

I like this recipe because the beef mixture is from a chuck roast, which is a nice change from ground beef, and serving them to my almost-adult sons makes them feel like kids again. Giant kids.

Makes 12 sliders

SLIDERS
2 tablespoons kosher salt
1½ teaspoons freshly ground black pepper
1 teaspoon ground cumin
1 teaspoon ground coriander
1 teaspoon smoked paprika
One 2-pound chuck roast
2 tablespoons extra virgin olive oil
1 yellow onion, quartered
4 garlic cloves, smashed
4 cups beef broth
1 cup ketchup
¼ cup apple cider vinegar
¼ cup light brown sugar
½ teaspoon ground mustard
½ teaspoon onion powder
1 teaspoon Worcestershire sauce

COLESLAW
¼ cup mayonnaise
1 tablespoon apple cider vinegar
¼ teaspoon celery seed
Kosher salt
Freshly ground black pepper
½ small head Savoy cabbage, thinly shredded
1 carrot, peeled and grated
2 scallions, white and green parts thinly sliced

12 slider buns, to serve

1. Position a rack in the center of the oven and preheat it to 325°F.
2. In a small bowl, combine the 2 tablespoons salt, 1 teaspoon pepper, the cumin, coriander, and paprika. Generously season both sides of the chuck roast with the spice rub.
3. Heat the oil in a large Dutch oven over medium-high heat. Add the roast and cook until nicely browned underneath, 3 to 5 minutes. Turn the roast over and cook until browned on the other side, 3 to 5 minutes more.

4. Remove the roast from the pot and place in a bowl. Add the onion and garlic to the Dutch oven and sauté for 5 minutes. Return the meat to the pot and add the beef broth. Bring the braising liquid to a boil and reduce to a simmer. Cover and roast in the oven for 2 to 2½ hours, until the meat is fork-tender.

5. While the beef is cooking, prepare the slaw: Combine the mayonnaise, 1 tablespoon vinegar, and celery seed in a large bowl. Season with salt and pepper and whisk to blend. Add the cabbage, carrot, and scallions and stir until well mixed. Set aside in the fridge until ready to serve.

6. Remove the pot roast to a large bowl and let it cool slightly. Shred the beef with two forks. (You can discard the braising liquid.)

7. Place the ketchup, ¼ cup vinegar, brown sugar, mustard, onion powder, Worcestershire sauce, and ½ teaspoon black pepper into a medium saucepan and whisk to combine. Simmer over medium heat for 10 minutes, then spoon the sauce over the shredded beef, tossing to coat it evenly.

8. Serve the beef family style with a platter of slider buns and coleslaw, or assemble the sliders if serving them for a party. Make sure to have small plates and plenty of napkins for serving. These sliders can be drippy!

SHORTCUTS

Feel free to use 1½ cups of your favorite store-bought BBQ sauce, or one of your own, in this recipe. Ditto for the coleslaw.

Falafel Patties with Tahini-Maple Dipping Sauce

When I was at Ohio State, we'd pour into the late-night falafel joint after all the bars had closed. I adore all that Middle Eastern food: falafel, hummus, baba ganoush.

These dippers are slightly flattened falafels, with their own cool dipping sauce.

Makes 4 appetizer servings

FALAFEL PATTIES
1 small yellow onion
1 garlic clove
One (19-ounce) can chickpeas, drained and rinsed
Handful of fresh flat-leaf parsley
½ teaspoon sea salt
Freshly ground black pepper
1 teaspoon ground cumin
½ teaspoon ground coriander
3 tablespoons all-purpose flour
Canola or grapeseed oil

DIPPING SAUCE
¼ cup tahini
¼ cup plain Greek yogurt
Juice of 1 lemon
1 teaspoon chopped fresh flat-leaf parsley leaves
½ teaspoon pure maple syrup
Sea salt and freshly ground black pepper

1. Make the falafel: Place the onion and garlic in the bowl of a food processor and pulse to roughly chop them. Add the chickpeas, parsley, salt, pepper, cumin, coriander, and flour. Pulse a few times, until just combined—the mixture should be a little chunky. Transfer to a bowl, cover, and chill in the fridge at least 4 hours and up to 2 days.

2. When ready to cook the falafel, shape the chilled mixture into 20 patties. They should be the size of sliders, or little hockey pucks, rather than balls.

3. Line a dish with paper towels. Heat ¼ inch of oil in a medium skillet over medium heat. Working in batches, fry the patties until deeply golden underneath, 2 to 3 minutes. Turn and cook on other side until deeply golden, 2 to 3 minutes more. Transfer to the paper towel–lined dish to drain.

4. Meanwhile, make the dipping sauce: Combine the tahini, yogurt, lemon juice, parsley, and syrup in a small bowl. Whisk until smooth and well blended, adding a few drops of water to thin out to the desired consistency. Season with salt and pepper.

5. Serve the hot falafel with the dipping sauce.

Pizza Monkey Bread

There's always lots of food on the set of a TV show, and monkey bread started sneaking its way onto the set of *The Middle* a few years ago. I love everything about it—the pulling apart, the chewiness, the fact that it's sometimes sweet and sometimes savory. Mmm . . . This is my version of monkey bread with a pizza flair. My boys love pizza . . . but who doesn't?

I make my own dough, but you could also start with 1 pound of prepared dough if you're pressed for time. ***Makes 12 servings***

1¾ cups all-purpose flour, plus more for kneading
1 teaspoon sea salt
½ teaspoon active dry yeast
¾ cup warm water (105°F to 110°F)

Cooking spray
1 cup jarred tomato-basil sauce
¾ cup grated Pecorino Romano
1¼ cups shredded mozzarella

1. Combine the flour, salt, yeast, and water in a large bowl. Stir until just combined and shaggy-looking. Turn the dough out onto a lightly floured counter. Knead until it becomes smooth and is no longer sticky, adding more flour only as needed. Cover the dough with a clean kitchen towel and let rest on the countertop until doubled in size, 1 to 1½ hours.
2. When the dough has risen, preheat the oven to 450°F. Generously coat an 11 × 7-inch baking dish with cooking spray.
3. Pluck off tablespoonfuls of dough and roll them into balls roughly the size of Ping-Pong balls.
4. Spread half the tomato sauce in the bottom of the baking dish. Sprinkle half the Pecorino Romano and half the mozzarella evenly over the sauce. Place the dough balls in the pan, giving them a snug fit. Spread the remaining sauce and cheeses over the dough balls.
5. Bake until puffed and golden, 35 to 40 minutes.

NO THERMOMETER?

Water is the correct temperature when it's warm enough to run across your wrist from the faucet without burning or stinging.

Buffalo Cauliflower Bites with Ranch Dipping Sauce

Cauliflower is the unsung hero of the vegetable world. Full of fiber and a great source of vitamin C, it's a graceful hostess, welcoming all other flavors to the mix. Cauliflower has the crunch of broccoli, but a milder taste, and there are a ton of things you can do with it. Here I've cut the cauliflower into little bites and baked it with a lovely coating. Dipping these babies in my tangy, spicy dip will make you forget you're being healthy.

Makes 4 appetizer servings

BUFFALO BITES
Cooking spray
½ cup all-purpose flour
½ teaspoon garlic powder
¼ teaspoon sea salt
½ teaspoon freshly ground black pepper
1 cauliflower head, trimmed and core discarded, florets cut into bite-size pieces
2 tablespoons unsalted butter, melted
¼ cup hot sauce (choose your favorite brand and heat level)

DIPPING SAUCE
¼ cup mayonnaise
¼ cup sour cream
2 tablespoons buttermilk
1 teaspoon lemon juice
Splash of apple cider vinegar
Handful of fresh chives, chopped
Sea salt and freshly ground black pepper

1. Preheat the oven to 450°F. Generously coat an 11 × 17-inch rimmed baking sheet with cooking spray.
2. Make the buffalo bites: Combine the flour, garlic powder, salt, pepper, and ½ cup of water in a large bowl. Add the cauliflower and toss until well coated. Arrange the cauliflower in a single layer in the prepared pan. Bake for 18 minutes, turning halfway through, until golden on both sides.
3. Meanwhile, whisk together the butter and hot sauce in a small bowl. Pour over the cauliflower, stirring to make sure it's well coated. Bake for 20 minutes more, turning halfway through, until crispy.
4. Make the dipping sauce: In a medium bowl, whisk together the mayonnaise, sour cream, buttermilk, lemon juice, and vinegar. Stir in the chives and season with salt and pepper.
5. Serve the hot cauliflower bites with the dipping sauce.

Watermelon and Feta Kabobs

These are a truly elegant summer treat, and great as appetizers at a pool party. The watermelon is naturally sweet, and cooling, while the feta offers a bit of zing. These are easy to make and if your guests are at the door, you can save time by using store-bought balsamic glaze rather than making your own.

Makes 10 appetizer servings, or 20 skewers

SPECIAL EQUIPMENT
Cocktail-size wooden skewers

¼ cup balsamic vinegar
1 small whole seedless watermelon

4 ounces feta cheese, finely crumbled
Handful of fresh mint, chopped

1. Bring the vinegar to a boil in a small pot over medium-high heat. Cook until reduced to 1½ tablespoons, 6 to 7 minutes.
2. Cut the watermelon in half and use a melon baller to scoop out the fruit. Place the watermelon balls in a colander or strainer to drain the juice.
3. Add 4 watermelon balls to each skewer (you'll need about 20 skewers). Arrange the skewers on a serving platter.
4. Sprinkle the skewers with the feta cheese and mint, drizzle the balsamic over the skewers, and serve immediately.

Bite-Size Crab Cakes with Lemon Aioli

The best thing about crab cakes is how they're crispy on the outside yet warm, soft, and meaty on the inside. And lemon aioli is their perfect mate. You can make the aioli at the same time as the crab cakes, or up to three days before serving, as long as it's refrigerated.

Don't be intimidated; these are easier to make than you might think. But beware: They'll disappear fast at your next cocktail party!

Makes 24 bite-size cakes, which will serve 12

CRAB CAKES
1 tablespoon unsalted butter
1 small yellow onion, chopped fine
¼ cup mayonnaise
1 large egg
2 teaspoons Dijon mustard
2 teaspoons Worcestershire sauce
Sea salt and freshly ground black pepper
Handful of fresh flat-leaf parsley leaves, chopped
½ cup panko bread crumbs
¼ cup all-purpose flour
Two 6-ounce cans lump crabmeat, picked over for shells (fresh crab is fine, too)
Canola oil

AIOLI
1 garlic clove, cut in half
½ cup mayonnaise
1 teaspoon Dijon mustard
Zest and juice of 1 lemon
1 teaspoon chopped chives
Sea salt and freshly ground black pepper

1. Make the crab cakes: Melt the butter in a small skillet over medium heat. Add the onion and sauté until lightly golden and softened, 2 to 3 minutes. Remove from the heat and set aside.

2. In a medium bowl, combine the mayonnaise, egg, Dijon, and Worcestershire. Season with salt and pepper and whisk to blend. Add the onion, parsley, bread crumbs, flour, and crabmeat. Stir to combine.

3. Line a plate with paper towels. Heat ¼ inch canola oil in a medium skillet over medium-high heat until shimmering. Using a 2-teaspoon cookie scoop, form the crab mixture into patties. Working in batches as needed, place the patties in the skillet. Cook until golden, flip, and cook until golden on other side, 5 to 6 minutes in total. Transfer to the paper towel–lined plate to drain.

4. Make the aioli: Rub the cut garlic clove around the inside of a medium bowl. Add the mayonnaise, mustard, and lemon zest and juice. Whisk to blend. Stir in the chives, season with salt and pepper to taste, and whisk again.

5. Spoon the aioli into a small bowl. Place in the center of a serving platter and arrange the crab cakes around it. Alternatively, you can arrange the crab cakes on a platter and spoon a small dollop of the aioli on top of each to serve as passed hors d'oeuvres.

A Glorious Cheese Board

A cheese board is like a painting; the board is the canvas and the foods are the colors.

No pressure.

But seriously, for you creative types, a cheese board offers plenty of opportunity for expression, and the kitchenware industry has driven the whole thing with cute, fun, and wholly impractical cheese boards. We've gone *way* beyond your mom's cutting board, my friend; you can now lay your spread on slate, stone, marble, and fifty different types of finished wood. It's a cheese board jungle out there!

As in life, the key to pulling together a show-stopping cheeseboard is balance. You want to have a good mix of savory, salty, crunchy, and sweet. Done well, a glorious cheeseboard like this can double as a rather filling meal. Many of the recipes in this book are anchors for a fabulous cheese board, so you'll see them listed below.

Makes as many servings as you like

Crispy Prosciutto Chips (page 82)
Quick Bread-and-Butter Pickles
   (page 84)
Toasted Walnut and Dried Cranberry
   Goat Cheese Log (page 80)

Rosemary Oyster Crackers (page 143)
   and/or other crackers
Selection of hard and soft cheeses
Assorted dried fruits and nuts
Selection of cured meats

Now let's break this down:

Cheese: Three varieties is a nice mix. A hard cheese, a soft cheese, and a cheese log is my standard. Go with what you like to eat, but be mindful that not everyone likes an assertive cheese, so make sure to include a mild one. As a guide, plan on 3 to 4 ounces of cheese in total per person.

Dried Fruits and Nuts: Including dried fruits and nuts covers your bases for the non-cheese eaters in the crowd. They're also the first part of the cheeseboard that kids will nibble away at. Some favorites include marcona almonds, pistachios, walnuts, dried sour cherries, dates, and apricots. Plan on a generous handful per person.

Cured Meats: Mortadella, salami, pepperoni—all winners, and sure to disappear quickly. Prosciutto is another favorite, and the Crispy Prosciutto Chips (page 82) are an easy way to add a wow factor. Allow 2 ounces of meat per person.

Toasted Walnut and Dried Cranberry Goat Cheese Log

This cheese log has a great combination of textures—between the crunch of the walnuts, the chewiness of the cranberries, and the smoothness of the goat cheese—not to mention a great mix of flavors. It's an elegant addition to A Glorious Cheese Board (page 79), and always a hit at a party. ***Makes 8 appetizer servings***

½ cup toasted walnuts, chopped fine (see "Toasting Nuts," page 43)
½ cup dried cranberries, chopped fine

½ teaspoon chopped fresh thyme leaves
Two 4.5-ounce goat cheese logs

1. Combine the walnuts, cranberries, and thyme on parchment paper or in a pie plate. Working one at a time, roll the goat cheese logs in the mixture, pressing gently to make sure the nuts and fruit stick to the cheese.
2. Wrap the logs tightly in plastic wrap and chill until ready to serve. These may be prepared up to 5 days in advance.

Crispy Prosciutto Chips

Prosciutto is a dry-cured ham from Italy that comes very thinly sliced. It tastes amazing with fresh fruit and cheese. Beyond a finger food, these chips are an alternate topping to Spicy Baked Avocado Eggs (page 45), or can be used to make the Glorious Cheese Board (page 79) even more glorious.

Makes 4 appetizer servings

One 3-ounce package thinly sliced prosciutto

1. Preheat the oven to 350°F. Line a baking sheet with parchment paper long enough to hang over the sides of the pan.
2. Arrange the slices of prosciutto on the prepared pan, making sure they don't overlap. Bake until crispy, about 25 minutes. Let cool a few minutes before serving. The chips may be prepared up to 4 hours in advance.

Epic Sheet Pan Nachos

I hate it when a plate of nachos has, like, eight chips with topping on them, lording it over a hundred naked chips. So I decided to remedy the situation with this layered-nacho trick. A platter of these babies is perfect for when all the boys are home, watching the game. Go Browns! *Makes 6 to 8 appetizer servings*

Cooking spray
¾ cup cooked shredded beef or pulled pork (Perfect Pot Roast, page 92, or Carnitas, page 132)
½ cup salsa verde (your favorite, jarred or canned, is fine) if using carnitas, plus more for drizzling
12 ounces tortilla chips (half a large, family-size bag)
12 ounces Cheddar cheese, shredded

1 cup canned black beans, drained and rinsed
1 avocado, halved, seeded, peeled, and cut into ¼- to ½-inch dice
2 plum tomatoes, cut into ¼- to ½-inch dice
Handful of fresh cilantro leaves, chopped
1 jalapeño, cut into thin rounds
Few dollops of sour cream, optional

1. Position a rack in the center of the oven and preheat it to 350°F. Coat a large baking sheet with cooking spray.
2. If using carnitas, combine the pork with the salsa verde until evenly coated.
3. Arrange half of the tortilla chips on the prepared baking sheet. Sprinkle with half of the cheese, the beef, and the beans. Repeat with the remaining chips, cheese, beef, and beans.
4. Bake 10 minutes, until the cheese is melted and the nachos are heated through.
5. As soon as the nachos are done, scatter the avocado, tomatoes, cilantro, jalapeño, salsa, and sour cream, if using, on top. Serve hot.

Quick Bread-and-Butter Pickles

Homemade pickles are easy to make and extremely delicious. They're all the rage these days, which is funny, because it's just one of those examples of everything old being new again. Pickling was necessary back in the day in order to preserve food, and it just happens that pickles are incredibly good for us, delivering vitamins and important bacteria to our guts.

I must confess I don't make them often, but I thought I'd try my hand at pickling, and it worked out very nicely. These are considered refrigerator pickles, because they are not meant for long-term storage on a shelf. I've included them here as a finger food, but they're also great to add to burgers or your cheese board. ***Makes about 3 pints***

SPECIAL EQUIPMENT

3 sterilized pint jars (see "How to Sterilize Glass Jars," opposite)

6 kirby cucumbers, cut into ¼-inch-thick coins
2 tablespoons coarse salt
1 cup apple cider vinegar

1 cup white vinegar
¾ cup pure maple syrup
2 teaspoons mustard seed
One ½-inch piece cinnamon stick
6 whole cloves
6 allspice berries
½ teaspoon ground turmeric

1. Place the cucumber slices in a large bowl, sprinkle with the salt, and toss well. Let stand for 30 minutes. Rinse and set aside in a colander or strainer.
2. To make the brine, in a deep pot over high heat, combine the apple cider vinegar, white vinegar, syrup, mustard seed, cinnamon stick, cloves, allspice, and turmeric. Bring to a boil, then reduce heat and simmer for 5 minutes. Add the cucumber slices and return to a boil. Reduce the heat to a simmer and cook 2 minutes more. Do not overcook or you'll end up with limp pickles.
3. Transfer the pickles to sterilized jars. These pickles will last for two months in the fridge. If you want to make a longer-term pickle, you should process the jars in a slightly more complicated hot water bath in order to seal them (Google it).

Roasted Butternut Squash and Garlic Dip

This simple, easy dish is great served with thin crackers, toasted slices of baguette, or raw vegetables for dipping. The squash and garlic make a satisfying combination, and you can adjust the seasoning to suit your taste. *Makes 6 to 8 servings*

1 medium butternut squash (about 2 pounds), peeled, seeded, and diced into 1-inch cubes
2 garlic cloves
Extra virgin olive oil
Sea salt and freshly ground black pepper

½ teaspoon ground cumin
1 tablespoon lime juice (from ½ small lime)
1 teaspoon honey
Handful of fresh cilantro leaves, chopped
2 tablespoons pomegranate seeds

1. Preheat the oven to 375°F.
2. Combine the squash and garlic in a 9 × 13-inch roasting pan and drizzle with olive oil. Season with salt, pepper, and cumin and toss to combine. Bake for 35 to 40 minutes, until the squash is very tender. Remove from the oven and set aside to cool for at least 10 minutes.
3. Add the squash, garlic, lime juice, and honey to the bowl of a food processor and pulse until smooth.
4. Spread the puree onto a serving plate. Drizzle a bit of olive oil on top. Scatter the cilantro and pomegranate seeds over the dip. Serve immediately.

HOW TO STERILIZE GLASS JARS

Wash the jars in hot, soapy water and rinse them with very hot water.

Place the jars on a rack set in a deep pot or a water-bath canner. Cover with water.

Over high heat, bring the water to a boil. Let the water boil for 15 minutes.

Right before you're ready to use the jars, lift the rack out of the pot (or use clean tongs) to place the jars upside down on a clean kitchen towel to dry.

The lids should be sterilized by boiling in water for 5 minutes.

Chutney Deviled Eggs

The world is your egg here, and I encourage you to experiment with mustards, herbs, spices, and other seasonings to find *your* perfect deviled egg. You little devil . . .

Makes 4 to 6 appetizer servings

6 large eggs
2 tablespoons mango chutney
3 tablespoons mayonnaise
1 teaspoon Dijon mustard

Few dashes of paprika
1 lemon wedge (¼ or ⅛ of a lemon)
Sea salt
Freshly chopped parsley, to garnish

1. Place the eggs in a pot just large enough to hold them snug. Fill the pot with water to fully cover the eggs. Bring to a boil over medium-high heat. Cover the pot with a lid and remove it from the heat. Let sit for 10 minutes.
2. Fill a bowl with water and ice cubes. Drain the eggs from the pot and add them to the bowl. Let sit for 5 minutes to cool. (At this point you can continue with the recipe or store the eggs in a container in the fridge for up to 3 days.)
3. Peel the eggs (see "Peeling Fabulous," below) and rinse them in a bowl of water to remove any shell particles. Gently pat dry with a towel.
4. Slice the eggs in half lengthwise. Gently scoop out the yolks. Slice a thin layer off the bottom of the egg whites so they sit flat, cut-side up, on a serving platter.
5. Place the chutney in the bowl of a food processor and pulse until smooth. Add the egg yolks, mayonnaise, mustard, and a dash of paprika. Squeeze in the lemon juice (no seeds!) and season with salt. Pulse until smooth.
6. Scrape the filling into a pastry bag (or a zip-top bag with a bottom corner cut off) and pipe it into the center of the egg whites. Add a few dashes of paprika on top and sprinkle the parsley over the deviled eggs. Serve immediately.

PEELING FABULOUS

After a boiled egg is cool to the touch, I tap it lightly on my kitchen counter until the shell is cracked all over. I then roll it on the counter gently, under my palm, to further crack the shell. Finally, I peel it, starting from the larger end of the egg.

Cashew and Coconut Shrimp

This is a spin on a recipe I created for my cooking show, *Patricia Heaton Parties*. I love the combination of hot, juicy shrimp with a crispy coating and a zingy dipping sauce. Delish.

Makes 18 shrimp, for 4 to 6 appetizer servings

½ cup mango peach jam
2 tablespoons white vinegar
¼ teaspoon red pepper flakes,
  or to taste
¾ cup raw cashews
¾ cup panko bread crumbs
¾ cup shredded, unsweetened
  coconut

½ cup all-purpose flour
½ teaspoon sea salt
Freshly ground black pepper
1 pound large shrimp (this will be
  about 18), shelled and deveined
Canola oil
2 large eggs, lightly beaten

1. Combine the jam, vinegar, and red pepper flakes in a small bowl. Stir to combine. Set aside in the fridge until ready to serve.
2. Place the cashews in a food processor and pulse to break them up a bit. Add the bread crumbs and coconut and pulse a few times just to combine.
3. In a large bowl, whisk together the flour, salt, and pepper. Add the shrimp and toss to coat.
4. In a large, deep skillet over medium heat, heat ¼ inch canola oil until shimmering.
5. Take a shrimp from the flour, shake off any excess, and dip it in the egg. Shake off any excess egg and dip the shrimp in the cashew mixture. Repeat with the remaining shrimp.
6. Fry the shrimp in the oil, turning once, until golden, and cooked through, 4 to 5 minutes, adding more oil to the pan as needed. Drain cooked shrimp on a wire rack.
7. Arrange cooked shrimp on a platter with the dipping sauce; serve immediately.

Comforting Classics

Ah, the classics. I created this chapter as an homage to my mother and her copy of the Better Homes and Gardens Cookbook, *with its red-and-white-checked cover. Between reading that and watching Julia Child, she picked up some classics—and some lovely comfort foods—that she passed on to me.*

However, because I married an Englishman, and have been lucky enough to travel the world a little more than my mother did, I've expanded our culinary territory in this chapter.

Here's to great food, and all the cooks who've cherished, and improved upon, these recipes.

Perfect Pot Roast

Growing up, my mother would make pot roast for a Sunday meal, or for when we had company; it's a lovely reminder of home.

Makes 4 servings

Sea salt and freshly ground black pepper
½ teaspoon ground fennel
One 3-pound chuck roast
Extra virgin olive oil
3 large carrots, peeled and cut into 2-inch-long chunks
½ pound cipollini onions, peeled, or 1 large Vidalia onion, cut into ¼- to ½-inch dice

3 garlic cloves, smashed
1¼ cups hard cider (or apple cider if you prefer nonalcoholic)
3½ cups beef broth
6 fresh thyme sprigs
1 fresh rosemary sprig
1 fresh or dried bay leaf
2 tablespoons all-purpose flour
2 tablespoons tomato paste

1. Preheat the oven to 325°F.
2. Combine the salt, pepper, and ground fennel in a small bowl. Generously season the roast with the spice mixture.
3. Add enough oil to a large Dutch oven to coat the bottom. Heat it over medium-high heat, add the roast, and sear 8 to 10 minutes total, turning to brown all sides. Transfer the roast to a bowl.
4. Add the carrots, onions, and garlic and season lightly with salt and pepper. Sauté the vegetables until browned, 5 to 8 minutes, being careful not to burn the garlic. Remove the vegetables and place in a clean bowl.
5. Deglaze the pot with 1 cup of the cider. Using a wooden spoon, scrape up any brown bits that have stuck to the bottom of the pot. Bring the liquid to a boil over high heat. Add 2 cups of the broth and bring it to a boil again.
6. Add 4 sprigs of the thyme, the rosemary, bay leaf, and roast to the pot (reserving the vegetables in the bowl). Bring the liquid to a boil, then reduce heat to a simmer.
7. Cover the pot, place it in the oven, and roast for 2 hours. Add the reserved vegetables and roast for 1 more hour, until the roast is fork-tender but not mushy.
8. Remove the roast and vegetables to a large bowl or platter and cover to keep warm. Let the braising liquid cool slightly, then strain the liquid into a bowl (discard the solids).
9. Skim off any fat that has risen to the top.

10. Purée the braising liquid in a blender.

11. To make the sauce, heat 2 tablespoons oil in the Dutch oven over medium heat. Add the flour and stir to combine with the oil. Stir in the remaining ¼ cup cider and the tomato paste and mix well.

12. Return the braising liquid to the pot along with the remaining 1½ cups beef broth and the remaining 2 thyme sprigs. Increase the heat to medium-high and bring to a boil. Reduce to a simmer and cook for 15 to 20 minutes, until the sauce is thickened.

13. Season the sauce with salt and pepper to taste. Remove the thyme sprigs.

14. To serve, slice the pot roast, arrange the vegetables around it, and pour the sauce over the top.

TIPSY POT ROAST

In many pot roast recipes, there is an element of alcohol. In mine, I use hard cider, but you can also try red wine, a heavy beer, or—for your Irish friends—Guinness. The booze gives the meat an extra dimension but won't get the family hammered.

Mom's Meatballs

Although she wasn't a natural cook, Mom did pass her meatballs on to me, and I remember mushing up the ground beef in my hands and forming it into the perfect shape. For this recipe, I've spruced the meatballs up with some Pecorino Romano cheese—not something she would have found at the Bay Village supermarket. This recipe also contains a quick and easy sauce, made from crushed tomatoes cooked in the oil and flavorings of the meatballs. If you're so inclined, serve on pasta, but meatballs can also be served with bread and a salad. Mamma mia! ***Makes 4 servings***

1 pound 85% lean ground beef,
   or a blend of pork and beef
½ cup 2% or whole milk, slightly
   warmed
½ cup plain bread crumbs
½ cup grated Pecorino Romano
Handful of fresh flat-leaf parsley
   leaves, chopped fine
1 small yellow onion, grated on
   the medium holes of box grater

1 large egg
Sea salt and freshly ground black
   pepper
Generous pinch of freshly grated
   nutmeg
Olive oil (canola or grapeseed oils
   work, too)
One (28-ounce) can crushed
   tomatoes
Handful of fresh basil leaves

1. Combine the beef, milk, bread crumbs, Pecorino Romano, parsley, onion, and egg in a deep bowl. Season with the salt, pepper, and nutmeg. Using clean hands, mix well to blend all the ingredients together.

2. Shape the mix into 20 balls (a medium cookie scoop is handy if you have one).

3. Heat ¼ to ½ inch of oil in a deep skillet over medium heat. Working in batches so as not to crowd the pan, fry the meatballs until nicely browned all around, 6 to 8 minutes. Transfer the cooked meatballs to a bowl.

4. Pour off all but 1 tablespoon of oil from the skillet (I pour it into an old coffee can, not down the drain). Stir the tomatoes into the oil, making sure to scrape up any browned bits from the bottom (they add flavor to the sauce). Season with salt and pepper and bring to a boil. Add the meatballs back to the pan and reduce the heat to low. Simmer, uncovered, for 20 minutes, or until the meatballs are cooked through.

5. Chop the basil and add it to the pan. Stir to combine with the sauce. Simmer for 2 minutes more. Serve hot.

Eggplant Parmigiana

The Italians really understand food, and this is a wonderful, classic dish from La Bella Italia. Eggplant parmigiana is good all year round, but I like it most in fall and winter, when everyone can come in from the cold and just spoon themselves a big, hot serving from the pan. Whenever we go skiing as a family, I always make sure to precook casseroles and other types of one-dish meals, so we can all relax and warm up after a day on the slopes without too much fuss. Eggplant parm is a family favorite. The best part is I can do the preparation ahead of time, even freeze it, and just stick it in the oven when I need to. It's also good the next day . . . sometimes better. ***Makes 4 to 6 servings***

Extra virgin olive oil
2 eggplants (about 1 pound each;
　　see "The Birds and the Bees of
　　Eggplants," below), cut into
　　¼-inch-thick slices

Cooking spray
1½ cups marinara sauce
1 cup grated Pecorino Romano
3 ounces mozzarella, shredded

1. Preheat the oven to 400°F.

2. Brush a bit of olive oil on two 11 × 17-inch baking sheets. Arrange the eggplant in a single layer on the baking sheets. Brush the tops with a bit more oil. Bake 20 to 25 minutes, turning halfway through, until tender and golden. (This can be done

THE BIRDS AND THE BEES OF EGGPLANTS

Just like there are girl and boy humans, there are girl and boy eggplants. Male eggplants are generally longer, often have a tightly closed "navel" (the spot at the butt), and contain fewer seeds. Female eggplants are rounder, often have looser navels, and contain many more seeds. Makes sense.

But with eggplants, the seed issue is important, because the seeds taste bitter. So, when it comes to eggplant parmigiana, boys get the job done better. If you find that you have chosen a lady eggplant at the store, you can remedy the bitterness situation by salting "her" for 30 minutes before proceeding with the recipe. Here's how: Layer the eggplant slices on a platter, salting each layer. Top with a dish and something to weigh it down. Let sit for 30 minutes. Rinse the eggplant to remove any excess salt, and pat dry. Proceed with the recipe as directed.

up to 2 days in advance. Let the eggplant cool, then store it in the fridge until
you're ready to finish the dish.)

3. Coat the bottom and sides of an 11 × 7½-inch baking dish with cooking spray.

4. Arrange the eggplant in a single layer, slightly overlapping each piece, in the bottom
of the pan. Spread ½ cup of sauce on top. Sprinkle ⅓ cup Pecorino Romano over
the sauce. Repeat to make two more layers of eggplant, sauce, and cheese.

5. Sprinkle the mozzarella on top and bake 20 minutes, until the cheese is melted
and lightly golden. Serve hot.

Spaghetti Bolognese

Okay, so Italian traditionalists will send me emails about serving Bolognese sauce over spaghetti (the purist serves it on tagliatelle or other flat pastas), but in the United States, *spaghetti* Bolognese has become a comforting classic. Although there are currently many versions, most boil down to beef cooked with finely chopped vegetables, to which milk is added and almost cooked away. This is a vital step, which gives the sauce its unique character. And it's so lovely.

Finally, some versions of Bolognese sauce contain bacon . . . can you guess which way I went on that?

Makes 4 servings

4 slices thick-cut bacon, chopped
1½ pounds 80% lean ground beef
Sea salt and freshly ground black
    pepper
Extra virgin olive oil
1 small carrot, peeled and chopped
    fine
1 small yellow onion, chopped fine
2 garlic cloves, minced

1 bay leaf
1¼ cups whole milk
½ cup dry red wine, such as
    cabernet sauvignon or merlot
One (28-ounce) can tomato
    puree
1 pound dried spaghetti
Grated Pecorino Romano,
    to serve, optional

1. Heat a deep pot over medium-high heat. Add the bacon and cook until crisp, 3 to 5 minutes. Use a slotted spoon to transfer to a large bowl. Add half of the beef to the pot and season with salt and pepper. Break up any large pieces with a fork or the back of a wooden spoon. Cook, stirring occasionally, until browned, 5 to 7 minutes. Use a slotted spoon to transfer the beef to the bowl with the bacon. Repeat with the remaining beef.

2. Add more oil to the pot if it seems too dry. Reduce heat to medium. Add the carrot and onion and season with salt and pepper. Cook, stirring once or twice, until the vegetables are softened and the onions are lightly golden, 2 to 3 minutes. Add the garlic to the carrot and onion and cook just until fragrant, 1 to 2 minutes. Add the bay leaf.

3. Return the meat and bacon to the pan and stir in the milk. Cook, stirring occasionally, until the milk has mostly evaporated but the meat is not dry, 10 to 12 minutes.

4. Stir in the wine, making sure to scrape up any browned bits from the bottom of the pan. Simmer for 2 minutes.

5. Stir in the tomato puree and season with salt. Bring to a boil, reduce heat to low, and cook, uncovered, for at least 2 hours, and up to 3 hours, stirring every 20 to 30 minutes. After 2 hours, the meat will be very tender and ready to eat, but if you give it the third hour, it will be that much more delicious (some Italian sauces are on the stove all day!). Add a few tablespoons of water as needed to prevent the sauce from sticking to the pan.

6. About 30 minutes before the sauce is done, begin preparing the pasta according to the package directions.

7. Remove the bay leaf and season the finished sauce with salt and pepper.

8. Drain the pasta and add it to the pot with the sauce. Stir until the pasta is well coated. Bring the pot to the table and serve family style, with Pecorino Romano, if using.

Chicken and Vegetable Cobbler

Dave and I were visiting London when I threw one of my first dinner parties as a married lady, and I must confess: I cheated. I snuck out to a famous butcher called C. Lidgate, one of the oldest butcher shops in the city, and I bought a chicken pot pie. Needless to say, it was delicious.

Since then, I've learned a thing or two about baking, and I love cobbler, a cousin to the traditional pot pie. It's a great family dish, served in the skillet right out of the oven, or you can make it in a pie plate to serve to guests at a casual party, with a big salad. It's warming and delicious and feels special. *Makes 2 to 4 servings*

FILLING
1 tablespoon unsalted butter
1 small, yellow onion, chopped fine
3 tablespoons all-purpose flour
¼ cup dry white wine, such as
    pinot grigio
1½ cups chicken broth
2 cups (8 ounces) cooked chicken,
    cut into ½-inch dice
1½ cups frozen peas and carrots
2 tablespoons heavy cream

BISCUIT TOPPING
1¼ cups all-purpose flour
2 teaspoons baking powder
½ teaspoon sugar
¼ teaspoon sea salt
3 tablespoons cold, unsalted butter,
    cut into 6 pieces
¾ cup cold heavy cream

1. Make the filling: Melt the butter in a medium (8-inch is good), ovenproof skillet over medium heat. Add the onion and sauté until lightly golden, about 2 minutes. Using a wooden spoon, stir in the flour. Cook for 1 minute.

2. Stir in the wine, breaking up any clumps of flour. Bring to a boil. Stir in the broth, chicken, and peas and carrots and bring to a boil. Stir in the cream and reduce the heat to low. Simmer until the sauce thickens enough to lightly coat the back of a spoon, about 10 minutes. The filling may still seem a bit soupy, but the biscuits will absorb some of the sauce while baking.

3. Preheat the oven to 425°F.

4. Meanwhile, prepare the biscuit topping: In a medium bowl, combine the flour, baking powder, sugar, and salt. Whisk to blend. Scatter the butter on top and use your fingers to rub it into the flour mixture. You should have some pebble-size bits, too. Stir in the cream just enough to form a rough dough.

5. Lightly dust a counter or cutting board with flour. Press the dough into a ½-inch-thick circle. Cut out biscuits using a 2½-inch cutter. Gently reroll the scraps and continue cutting out circles to use up the dough.

6. Arrange the biscuits on top of the filling in the skillet. Don't worry if there are some gaps; the biscuits will spread out during baking. Bake until the biscuits are golden and cooked through, 18 to 20 minutes. Serve hot out of the pan.

SINGLE SERVINGS, ANYONE?

If you'd like to make this dish in individual ramekins, you may be able to take a few minutes off the cooking time, but not more. The cooking time is for baking the biscuits, and volume doesn't affect the baking time too much. Check them at 15 minutes to test for doneness. Conversely, if you'd like to double the recipe, add 3 or 4 minutes to the baking time.

Bangers and Mash

When Dave and I were in England recently, we went to a pub in rainy London for Sunday brunch with friends. When ordering, we all indulged in one classic or another: Dave had cottage pie, our friends split fish 'n' chips, and I ordered the bangers and mash. It was pure heaven tucking into this dish with a beer, watching the "footy" (soccer) on the telly. There's a reason it's a classic.

And as much as I'm a fan of shortcuts, there's nothing better than homemade mashed potatoes, so don't skimp on them. And please don't make the mistake I once made by putting them in a blender, which created a gelatinous and paste-like substance, perfect for fixing a wall. Be sure to use a potato masher or ricer.

Makes 4 servings

3 russet potatoes (about 3 pounds), peeled and cut into 1-inch cubes
Sea salt
8 pork sausages (English-style bangers or Cumberland)
Extra virgin olive oil
2 shallots, thinly sliced
2 tablespoons thyme leaves

Freshly ground black pepper
2 tablespoons all-purpose flour
½ cup dry red wine, such as cabernet sauvignon or merlot
1½ cups beef broth
4 tablespoons (½ stick) unsalted butter
1 cup whole milk

1. Place the potatoes in a medium saucepan and fill with enough cold water to cover the potatoes by 1 inch. Add 1 tablespoon salt and bring to a boil over medium-high heat. Reduce the heat to medium and cook until the potatoes are very tender when pierced with a fork, 10 to 15 minutes.

2. Make small cuts along the length of each sausage on both sides, so that the casings don't tear while cooking.

3. Heat a large skillet over medium-high heat and swirl enough oil into the pan to cover the bottom. Add the sausages and cook, turning occasionally, until browned all over, 8 to 10 minutes. Transfer to a dish. Carefully remove all but 2 tablespoons of fat from the pan.

4. Reduce the heat to medium. Add the shallots and thyme and sauté until softened, 2 to 3 minutes. Season well with salt and pepper.

5. Sprinkle the flour into the pan. Stir, scraping up any browned bits. Add the wine and whisk to incorporate. The shallots will immediately absorb the liquid. Slowly whisk in the broth and turn the heat to medium-low. Cook, stirring occasionally, until the sauce has thickened slightly (enough to cling to the back of a spoon), 10 minutes. Taste and season with salt and pepper. Strain the gravy, discarding the solids, and return it to the skillet to keep warm.

6. Place the butter and milk in a small saucepan over medium-low heat, melting the butter into the milk. Keep warm over low heat.

7. Drain the potatoes in a colander and immediately return them to the pot. Place over low heat to evaporate any remaining moisture. Turn off the heat and pour in the warmed milk mixture. Using a potato masher, mash the potatoes until smooth. Season with salt and pepper.

8. Return the sausages to the pan, turn the heat to low, and simmer gently to heat the sausages and gravy. Divide the potatoes among four dishes, top each with 2 sausages, and spoon gravy over the sausages. Serve immediately.

Hearty Lamb Stew

I know that lamb stew sounds Irish, but I decided to put a spin on a classic Italian stew called *spezzatino*. The meat starts out in a cold pan—no browning necessary—and there's no flour, as the stew thickens on its own. This dish is great with a glass of red wine and, like lasagna, it's almost better the next day.

Makes 4 servings

One (28-ounce) can whole peeled plum tomatoes
2 teaspoons ground cumin
1 teaspoon ground coriander
1 teaspoon ground ginger
½ teaspoon ground cinnamon
1 teaspoon smoked paprika
2 tablespoons kosher salt, plus more to taste
1 teaspoon freshly ground black pepper, plus more to taste
2 pounds lamb shoulder or top round, cut into 2-inch cubes (your butcher can do this)

2 tablespoons extra virgin olive oil
1 medium onion, chopped
3 medium carrots, peeled and cut into 1-inch chunks
3 garlic cloves, chopped
2 tablespoons tomato paste
½ cup dry red wine, such as cabernet sauvignon
1 cup beef stock
1 bay leaf
1 large russet potato, peeled and cut into ½-inch cubes

1. Place the tomatoes in a large bowl and squeeze them between your fingertips to crush them roughly. Set aside with the juices.
2. Combine the cumin, coriander, ginger, cinnamon, smoked paprika, salt, and pepper in a medium bowl. Add the lamb and toss to evenly coat.
3. In a large Dutch oven, heat the olive oil over medium-high heat. Add the lamb and cook, stirring occasionally, until all sides of the lamb are seared, 5 to 7 minutes. Remove the browned lamb to a bowl and set aside.
4. Add the onion, carrots, and garlic to the Dutch oven and season with salt and pepper. Cook, stirring occasionally, until the onions are translucent, about 6 minutes.

5. Add the tomato paste and stir to incorporate. Pour in the wine and scrape up the brown bits stuck to the bottom of the pot. Cook for 2 minutes, then return the lamb and its juices to the pot. Add the stock, tomatoes, and bay leaf and season once again with salt and pepper. Bring the mixture to a boil, then lower the heat to a simmer. Cover and cook for 1 hour, stirring once or twice as needed.

6. Stir the stew, taste it for seasoning, and add more salt and pepper if desired. Scatter the potatoes on top, cover the pot, and simmer for 1 hour more, until the lamb is very tender and flakes with a fork. Discard the bay leaf and serve the stew hot.

David's Cottage Pie

The Brits love their pies, even though cottage pie isn't really a pie—it consists of mashed potatoes laid on top of ground beef and vegetables, all browned up and juicy. The better-known shepherd's pie is the same deal but contains some lamb. Both were developed as simple ways to use leftovers and yet are weirdly fantastic. We eat them all the time in our house.

Makes 4 servings

3 russet potatoes (about 3 pounds), peeled and cut into 1-inch cubes
Extra virgin olive oil
1½ pounds 85 or 90% lean ground beef
1 medium yellow onion, chopped fine
2 carrots, peeled and diced fine
1 celery rib, diced fine
1 cup fresh or frozen peas
¼ cup port (I prefer tawny but ruby works, too)

1 tablespoon Worcestershire sauce
2 tablespoons all-purpose flour
1½ cups beef broth
4 tablespoons (½ stick) unsalted butter
¼ to ½ cup 2% or whole milk, warmed
Sea salt
Freshly ground black pepper

1. Place the potatoes in a medium saucepan and add water to cover the potatoes by 1 inch. Bring to a boil over medium-high heat. Reduce the heat to medium and cook until the potatoes are very tender when pierced with a fork, 10 to 15 minutes.
2. Preheat the oven to 400°F.
3. While the potatoes cook, pour enough oil into a large skillet to coat the bottom and heat over medium-high heat until shimmering. Add the beef and cook, breaking up any large clumps with the back of a fork, until the meat is browned, 8 to 10 minutes. Transfer to a large bowl.
4. Add another swirl of oil into the pan, if needed. Add the onion, carrots, celery, and peas and sauté (still over medium-high heat) until slightly softened, 1 to 2 minutes.
5. Return the beef to the pan and add the port and Worcestershire. Cook for 1 minute. Sprinkle in the flour and stir to coat everything. Stir in the broth and turn the heat to medium-low. Cook for 5 minutes, until the filling begins to thicken slightly.

6. When the potatoes are cooked, drain them in a strainer. Return the potatoes to the saucepan and add the butter and milk. Season with salt and pepper. Smash the potatoes with a handheld potato masher until smooth; set aside.

7. Spoon the filling into a 9 × 13-inch ovenproof casserole dish and spread the potatoes evenly over the filling. Bake until the potatoes are golden and the filling is bubbling, about 30 minutes. For a nicely browned topping, you can finish by placing the dish under the broiler for 1 to 2 minutes, watching it carefully. Serve hot.

General Tso's Shrimp

There's nothing like the sweet and spicy taste of a General Tso sauce. A classic combination of flavors and textures, it never gets boring, and now you can make it at home!

Makes 4 servings

1 large egg white
¼ cup soy sauce
¼ cup sherry
½ cup plus 2 tablespoons cornstarch
1 pound extra-large shrimp (26/30 count bag), shelled and deveined
½ teaspoon baking powder
¼ teaspoon baking soda
½ teaspoon sea salt
Canola oil
2 garlic cloves, chopped fine

One 1-inch piece of ginger, peeled and chopped fine
1 scallion, thinly sliced (white and light green parts only)
¼ teaspoon crushed red pepper flakes
6 tablespoons vegetable or chicken broth
3 tablespoons sugar
1 teaspoon sesame oil
Cooked rice, for serving, optional

1. Beat the egg white in a large bowl until foamy. Add 2 tablespoons of the soy sauce, 2 tablespoons of the sherry, and 1 tablespoon of the cornstarch. Whisk to blend. Add the shrimp to the bowl. Cover and refrigerate for 15 minutes.

2. Combine the ½ cup cornstarch, the baking powder, baking soda, and salt in a shallow bowl. Whisk to blend.

3. Line a plate with paper towels. Fill a deep skillet with ¼ inch canola oil. Heat until shimmering. Working one piece at a time, take a shrimp from the marinade, shaking off any excess liquid, dredge it through the flour mixture, then add to the hot oil. Cook, turning once, until lightly golden and crisp, 2 to 3 minutes. Transfer to the paper towel–lined plate to drain. Repeat until all the shrimp are cooked.

4. Heat 2 teaspoons of the canola oil in a second large skillet over medium heat. Add the garlic, ginger, scallions, and red pepper flakes and sauté until fragrant and softened, about 2 minutes.

5. In a small bowl, combine the remaining 2 tablespoons soy sauce and 2 tablespoons sherry, the broth, sugar, sesame oil, and remaining 1 tablespoon cornstarch and whisk until blended and smooth. Stir the sauce into the garlic-ginger mixture. Bring to a boil, then cook for 1 minute. Remove the pan from the heat and stir in the shrimp. Serve hot, with rice, if desired.

Chicken Chilaquiles

Chilaquiles is a traditional Mexican dish, often served at breakfast or brunch. It usually consists of corn tortillas covered in a salsa, mixed with meat, and topped with cheese or sour cream—kind of like nachos made into a whole meal. We make chilaquiles in our household because it's fast, easy, and delicious. It's also a great solution to leftover chicken.

Makes 4 servings

2 teaspoons extra virgin olive oil
1 small yellow onion, chopped
1 garlic clove, chopped
1 (28-ounce) can crushed tomatoes
¼ cup pickled jalapeños, chopped
Sea salt
3 cups shredded leftover chicken

Generous handful of fresh cilantro leaves, chopped
4 ounces queso fresco or feta, crumbled
4 ounces corn tortilla chips
1 lime, cut into quarters

1. Heat the oil in a deep skillet over medium heat. Add the onion and sauté until lightly golden, about 2 minutes. Add the garlic and sauté until just softened but not browned, about 1 minute. Stir in the tomatoes and jalapeños and season with salt. Bring to a boil, then turn the heat to low and simmer for 10 minutes.
2. Stir in the chicken and most of the cilantro (save a little to garnish) and cook for 10 minutes more, until the chicken is heated through and the sauce has thickened.
3. Divide the chips among four deep bowls. Ladle the chicken over the chips. Top with cheese, the remaining cilantro, and a squeeze of lime. Serve immediately.

Crispy Fish Sticks

This is my homage to Mrs. Paul's fish sticks, which we ate every Friday night in Bay Village. It's a culinary tribute to Catholicism, my mother, and kids everywhere—like mine—who like to eat with their fingers. This recipe is easy and delicious, and although the breading is much lighter than you'll find in a traditional English fish 'n' chips, it's a good way to keep the calories down. Serve with French fries, obviously. ***Makes 4 servings***

TARTAR SAUCE
¼ cup mayonnaise
1 tablespoon chopped dill pickle
1 teaspoon brine-packed capers
(minced, if large)

FISH STICKS
1 pound cod, preferably a thick center-cut piece
¼ cup all-purpose flour
Sea salt and freshly ground black pepper
1 large egg
1¼ cups panko bread crumbs
Canola oil

1. Make the tartar sauce: Combine the mayonnaise, pickle, and capers in a small bowl. Stir to blend. Chill at least 1 hour and up to 3 days.
2. Make the fish sticks: Cut the cod into 12 sticks.
3. In a shallow bowl, season the flour with salt and pepper. In a separate shallow bowl, lightly whisk the egg. Place the panko in a third bowl.
4. Press a piece of fish into the flour and coat it all over, shaking off any excess. Dip the fish into the egg, shaking off any excess. Press firmly into the panko, making sure it's coated all over. Set the fish on a platter and repeat to coat the remaining fish sticks.
5. Line a plate with paper towels. In a medium skillet over medium-high heat, heat ¼ inch of oil until shimmering. Add the fish, turning as needed, until golden all over, 5 to 7 minutes (you may need to work in batches so as not to overcrowd the pan). Transfer to a paper towel–lined plate to drain. Serve hot with the prepared tartar sauce.

Spinach and Feta Toad-in-the-Hole

The classic toad-in-the-hole is a British dish, the first version of which was found in a cookbook from 1747. It's generally a sausage nestled within a Yorkshire pudding batter (egg, flour, milk) and baked. The sausage is the toad, and it's sort of poking out the "hole" of the pastry. . . . It's a bit odd, but I learned very early not to mess around with the Brits and their traditions.

My recipe uses fancy sausage made with spinach and feta, but you can use any kind you like. This is a nice dish for brunch, or lunch, and goes well with a gravy.

Makes 4 servings, with 1½ cups gravy

TOADS-IN-THE-HOLE
8 spinach and feta sausages (or any kind you like)
⅔ cup all-purpose flour
1¼ cups 2% or whole milk
1 large egg
½ teaspoon sea salt

GRAVY
2 tablespoons unsalted butter
1 medium carrot, peeled and roughly chopped

1 small yellow onion, roughly chopped
2 garlic cloves, chopped fine
1 tablespoon tomato paste
2 tablespoons all-purpose flour
½ cup dry vermouth (or dry white wine)
2 teaspoons Worcestershire sauce
1½ cups beef stock
2 teaspoons kosher salt
Freshly ground black pepper

1. Place a 12-inch cast-iron skillet on the center rack of the oven. Preheat the oven to 400°F.

2. Make the toads-in-the-hole: Cook the sausages in the skillet until nicely browned, 12 to 15 minutes, turning once.

3. Meanwhile, combine the flour, milk, egg, and salt in a medium bowl. Whisk until mixed well.

4. When the sausages are browned, arrange them any way you like (I line them up into straight rows) and pour the batter into the hot pan, over the sausages. Return the skillet to the oven and cook until the batter is puffed up and golden, about 30 minutes.

5. Make the gravy: In a medium saucepan over medium-high heat, melt the butter. Add the carrot, onion, and garlic and sauté until the onion is translucent, about 5 minutes. Add the tomato paste and stir to incorporate fully. Add the flour and stir. Add the vermouth and stir, scraping up any bits on the bottom of the pan. Whisk in the Worcestershire and stock, and season with salt and pepper. Bring the mixture to a boil, then reduce the heat to a high simmer and cook for 10 minutes, stirring often, until the gravy is thickened and coats the back of a spoon. Strain out the solids and discard. Return the gravy to low heat to keep warm. Adjust the seasoning if desired.

6. To serve, spoon sausage and pudding into shallow bowls. Cover with gravy and enjoy.

WHY PRINCE EDWARD ISLAND MUSSELS?

I find these to be the most consistent in flavor, and they always come cleaned and debearded. If you use another type of mussel, you may need to scrub them and remove the thin, sticky membranes known as "beards" that the mussels use to attach to stable surfaces.

Shortcut Paella

Dave and I went to Barcelona recently, and I had the *best* paella I've ever tasted. Of course, I came home and promptly bought a traditional paella pan, the rice, and a Spanish cookbook and started experimenting. My paella takes the shortcut of using day-old rice, which works really nicely and becomes sort of crispy. I also use turmeric instead of saffron for that bright, yellow color; it has a nice flavor, is ridiculously good for you, and is much cheaper than saffron.

Makes 4 servings

4 slices bacon, chopped
Extra virgin olive oil
1 green bell pepper, cut into ¼-inch dice
1 celery rib, chopped fine
1 small yellow onion, chopped fine
1 garlic clove, chopped fine
½ teaspoon ground turmeric
1 cup frozen peas
¼ cup dry white wine, such as pinot grigio

4 cups leftover cooked rice
Sea salt and freshly ground black pepper
½ pound large (31/35 count bag) shrimp, peeled and deveined
8 sea scallops (roughly ¾ pound)
1 pound Prince Edward Island (or other) mussels
Handful of cilantro leaves, roughly chopped, optional

1. Line a plate with paper towels. In a large nonstick skillet over medium heat, cook the bacon until crisp. Use a slotted spoon to transfer it to the paper towel–lined plate to drain.

2. Add the bell pepper, celery, and onion to the pan and sauté until slightly softened, about 2 minutes. Add the garlic, turmeric, and peas and sauté for 1 minute. Stir in the wine and cook for 1 minute more.

3. Place the rice in the skillet. Season with salt and pepper and stir to combine everything in the pan. Arrange the shrimp and scallops on top of the rice. Cover with a lid and cook for 5 minutes. Add the mussels to the pan, cover, and keep cooking until the shrimp and scallops are cooked through, the mussels have opened (discard any that do not), and the rice is slightly crispy on the bottom, 5 to 6 minutes more.

4. Sprinkle the bacon and cilantro, if using, on top. Serve hot.

Family Favorites

Every family develops habits and routines; without them, there would be chaos.

Well, more chaos.

These are some of the tried-and-true dishes I've made in our household over the years that make my whole brood happy. Well, most of the brood. It's hard to nail it every time with six people!

I hope these can become some of your family favorites, too.

Stuffed Shells

Ricotta is one of my favorite foods. I find its mild flavor and smooth texture enchanting. I especially love the moment I cut into a stuffed shell and the ricotta squirts out one side. It just makes me happy.

Stuffed shells are a people-pleasing classic, and a family favorite. If you'd like to give them a twist, try adding chopped roasted peppers to the filling, or top them with leftover Bolognese sauce. You can even swap in 1 cup of feta for part of the ricotta cheese.

Don't forget to eat your shells with salad, some nice, crispy Italian bread, and a good glass of wine. *Buon appetito!*   **Makes 8 servings**

One 12-ounce box jumbo shell pasta
4 cups ricotta cheese
2 large eggs
Generous handful of flat-leaf parsley, destemmed and chopped

1¾ cups grated Pecorino Romano
Sea salt and freshly ground black pepper
4 cups marinara sauce

1. Cook the shells al dente according to the package directions.
2. Preheat the oven to 375°F.
3. In a large bowl, combine the ricotta, eggs, parsley, and Pecorino Romano. Season with salt and pepper. Whisk to blend. Spoon the filling into a pastry bag or a zip-top bag with a corner snipped off.
4. Spread 2 cups of sauce in a 9 × 13-inch baking dish. Fill the shells with the cheese mixture and nestle them in the sauce cheese side up, snug in the dish. Spoon the remaining sauce over the top of the shells.
5. Bake 35 minutes, or until the sauce is bubbling. Serve hot.

THE SHELL GAME

If this recipe makes too much for one night, use two 8-inch square pans and bake one now and cover and freeze the other for later. When you're in the mood, just thaw the pan in the fridge overnight and bake as directed in the recipe.

Apricot-Glazed Pork Cutlets

This is a nice way of cooking pork so that it stays juicy, tender, and really flavorful. The sweetness of the apricot is the perfect complement to the meat, and they both go well with a simple side, like rice or quinoa.

Makes 4 servings

8 small boneless pork cutlets
   (about 3 ounces each)
1 teaspoon sea salt, plus more
   to taste
½ teaspoon freshly ground black
   pepper, plus more to taste

Extra virgin olive oil
1 shallot, chopped fine
½ cup dry white wine, such as
   pinot grigio
¾ cup apricot jam
Pinch of ground cloves

1. Season the pork all over with the salt and pepper.
2. Heat a large skillet over medium-high heat. Swirl in enough oil to coat the bottom of the pan. Working in batches as needed, add the cutlets and cook until browned underneath, 2 to 3 minutes. Turn the cutlets over and cook until browned on the other side, about 2 minutes more. Transfer the pork to a platter.
3. Reduce the heat to medium and add the shallot to the pan. Season with salt and pepper. Sauté until slightly softened and golden, about 2 minutes.
4. Stir in the wine and use a spoon or spatula to scrape up any browned bits from the bottom of the pan. Cook 2 to 3 minutes, until the wine has reduced by about one third. Stir in the jam and cloves and cook for 1 minute. Season with salt and pepper.
5. Return the pork to the pan, along with any juices that have collected in the dish. Stir the sauce to coat the cutlets. If the sauce seems too thick, stir in 2 to 3 tablespoons of water to thin it out to your liking.
6. Arrange the pork on a large, clean platter. Spoon the sauce over the cutlets and serve immediately.

Chicken Cutlets with Mushroom-Sage Sauce

You can see from this book that I like chicken. My whole family does. I generally have a chicken staring out at me from the refrigerator at all times. Here is a lovely way to cook chicken cutlets with a lip-smacking sauce.

Makes 6 servings

CHICKEN CUTLETS

1 cup all-purpose flour
1 teaspoon kosher salt, plus more to taste
½ teaspoon freshly ground black pepper, plus more to taste
3 large eggs
2 cups panko bread crumbs
6 butterflied chicken cutlets
Extra virgin olive oil

MUSHROOM-SAGE SAUCE

Extra virgin olive oil
1 small yellow onion, diced
Salt and freshly ground black pepper
8 ounces cremini mushrooms, sliced
2 garlic cloves, minced
8 sage leaves, chopped
Zest and juice of 1 lemon
½ cup dry white wine, such as sauvignon blanc or pinot grigio
4 ounces mascarpone cheese
3 tablespoons minced chives
Shaved Parmesan cheese, for garnish, optional

1. Preheat the oven to 200°F.
2. Make the chicken: Set up a breading station: In a medium bowl, place the flour, salt, and pepper. Whisk to combine. In a separate medium bowl, beat the eggs. In a third medium bowl, place the panko bread crumbs.
3. Dredge a chicken cutlet in flour. Shake off the excess flour and then submerge in the egg, shaking off any excess. Dredge in the panko, coating the cutlet well. Transfer to a baking sheet and repeat with the remaining cutlets.
4. Heat 3 tablespoons olive oil in a large skillet over medium heat. Working in batches as needed, add the breaded cutlets and cook for 3 minutes per side, until golden brown, crispy, and cooked through. Immediately season with salt and pepper. Remove the cutlets to a clean baking sheet and place them in the oven to keep warm.

5. Prepare the sauce: Carefully clean out the pan of any burned bits. Heat a drizzle of olive oil over medium-high heat, add the onion, and season with salt and pepper. Sauté for 3 to 5 minutes, until softened and lightly browned. Add the mushrooms (and more oil, if the pan is dry) and season with salt and pepper. Cook for 5 to 7 minutes, until the mushrooms are tender. Add the garlic and sage and cook just until fragrant, 1 to 2 minutes. Add the lemon zest and deglaze the pan with the lemon juice and wine. Cook for 3 minutes, then remove from the heat. Stir in the mascarpone cheese.

6. To serve, arrange the chicken on a platter and spoon the mushroom sauce on top. Garnish with the chives and shaved Parmesan cheese, if desired.

Lemon and Rosemary Roasted Chicken

The running joke on *Everybody Loves Raymond* was that everyone secretly thought that Debra (my character) was a lousy cook. But Debra's signature dish, of which she was very proud, was lemon chicken. I can't vouch for Debra's bird, but mine is fantastic and goes great with roasted potatoes and carrots.

Makes 4 servings

3½- to 4-pound whole chicken
Sea salt and freshly ground black
   pepper
1 lemon

Two 4-inch fresh rosemary sprigs
½ cup dry white wine, such as
   pinot grigio
2 tablespoons unsalted butter

1. Preheat the oven to 425°F.
2. Place the chicken in a 9 × 13-inch roasting pan or large cast-iron skillet, breast-side up, and season generously with salt and pepper. Slice the lemon into quarters and stuff the lemon wedges and rosemary sprigs inside the chicken cavity.
3. Roast for 20 minutes. Add the wine, butter, and ¾ cup water to the bottom of the pan. Roast for 40 minutes more, basting the chicken with the pan sauce every 10 to 15 minutes, until the juices run clear and an instant-read thermometer inserted in the thigh registers 165°F.
4. Let the chicken sit for 5 to 10 minutes before carving.

Creamy Turkey and Vegetable Soup

We love leftovers from Thanksgiving and Christmas feasts, but we don't stop at turkey sandwiches. Here is a lovely, creamy turkey soup that can extend your holiday joy another day or two. For other times of the year, use leftover chicken! *Makes 4 servings*

1 tablespoon extra virgin olive oil
1 small yellow onion, cut into
 ½-inch dice
6 shiitake mushrooms, stems
 discarded, caps cut into
 ¼-inch slices
Sea salt and freshly ground black
 pepper
2 carrots, peeled and cut into
 ½-inch dice
1 celery rib, cut into ½-inch dice
1 garlic clove, crushed

1 russet potato, peeled and cut
 into ½-inch dice
4 cups turkey or chicken broth
2 cups ½-inch-diced cooked turkey
1 bay leaf
½ cup heavy cream
1½ teaspoons all-purpose flour
Handful of fresh flat-leaf parsley
 leaves, chopped
Rosemary Oyster Crackers
 (page 143)

1. In a medium saucepan over medium-low heat, heat the oil until shimmering. Add the onion and mushrooms and season with salt and pepper. Sauté until softened and lightly golden, about 2 minutes.
2. Add the carrots, celery, and garlic and sauté 1 minute, until the garlic is fragrant.
3. Add the potatoes, broth, turkey, and bay leaf and season with salt and pepper. Increase the heat to high and bring to a boil. Reduce the heat to low and simmer until the potatoes are tender when pierced with a fork, about 10 minutes.
4. Combine the cream and flour in a small bowl and whisk until smooth. Stir the mixture into the soup and add the parsley. Let simmer for 5 minutes, then discard the bay leaf.
5. Ladle the soup into deep bowls and serve hot with Rosemary Oyster Crackers.

Lemon and Olive Baked Halibut

Fish can be tricky. I find that baking it takes the fishy edge off a little bit, so this recipe goes down well in my household. Plus, I'm a huge lover of anything with lemons and olives. You'll find that the parchment paper presentation makes this dish very easy and allows you to season each serving individually if you like, and you'll look like a total rock star when you serve the elegant parchment packets onto plates. For a light and elegant combination, try this with the Warm Quinoa, Shiitake, and Feta Salad on page 138, but skip the feta; cheese and fish don't pair very well. ***Makes 4 servings***

4 (6-ounce) halibut fillets
Sea salt and freshly ground black
 pepper
1 tablespoon plus 1 teaspoon extra
 virgin olive oil
¼ cup pitted kalamata and picholine
 olives, roughly chopped

8 fresh thyme sprigs
1 tablespoon plus 1 teaspoon
 pine nuts, toasted (see "Toasting
 Nuts," page 43)
1 lemon, cut into quarters

1. Preheat the oven to 400°F. Cut four 15-inch squares of parchment paper.
2. Place a piece of halibut in the center of each piece of parchment. Drizzle 1 teaspoon of the olive oil on top. Scatter 1 tablespoon of the olives over the fish and place 2 thyme sprigs on top. Fold the packet as if wrapping a gift, making sure the ends are folded tightly shut. Repeat with the remaining fillets.
3. Place the packets on a rimmed baking sheet and bake 15 minutes.
4. Transfer the packets to dinner plates, very carefully slice them open with a knife or scissors (steam will escape!), and sprinkle 1 teaspoon of pine nuts on top of each. Finish with a squeeze of lemon. Serve hot.

Skillet Steak with Red Wine Sauce and Mushrooms

I love steak; it always tastes good, and feels . . . special. In all the great steakhouses, they offer a variety of fancy sauces to complement their meat, and for a long time, I assumed they were difficult to make, but they're not! So take the time to throw together this sauce after cooking the steak and you will be very impressed with yourself. Your family and friends will be, too. P.S. This steak-sauce combination loves to be served with mashed potatoes or parsnips.

Makes 4 servings

STEAK

1½ pounds sirloin steak
Sea salt and freshly ground black pepper
Extra virgin olive oil

RED WINE SAUCE

8 ounces white button, crimini, or baby bella mushrooms, cut into ¼-inch-thick slices
1 shallot, cut into ⅛-inch rings
¼ cup dry red wine, such as cabernet sauvignon (or ¼ cup additional broth)
1½ tablespoons unsalted butter
1 teaspoon all-purpose flour
½ cup beef broth

1. Season both sides of the steak with salt and pepper.
2. Heat a cast-iron skillet over medium-high heat. Swirl in enough oil to coat the bottom of the pan. Add the steak to the skillet and cook, undisturbed, until nicely browned underneath, about 5 minutes. Turn and cook on the other side 3 minutes more for medium-rare. Transfer to a cutting board and cover loosely with a piece of foil.
3. Prepare the sauce: Reduce the heat to medium. Add the mushrooms and shallots and sauté until the mushrooms are golden and the shallots tender, 3 to 4 minutes.
4. Pour the wine into the pan and let it boil until slightly reduced, about 1 minute. Add the butter and stir until it has melted. Whisk the flour into the sauce until it is smooth and lump-free. Slowly whisk in the broth and season with salt and pepper. Cook 2 to 3 minutes, until the sauce thickens slightly.
5. Cut the steak into slices and arrange them on a serving platter. Spoon the mushrooms, shallots, and sauce over the top. Serve immediately.

Carnitas Taco Salad

Carnitas, meaning "little meats," is shredded pork, browned until slightly crispy. Mmm . . . Although the pork is done in a slow cooker and takes some time, the salad is a fresh take on Mexican cuisine. It's perfect for a summer day with Dave and the kids.

Makes 6 servings

CARNITAS
1 teaspoon sea salt
1 teaspoon ground cumin
1 teaspoon ground coriander
1 teaspoon dried oregano
2½ pounds pork shoulder
1 small yellow onion, cut into quarters
2 garlic cloves, smashed
½ cup orange juice, preferably freshly squeezed
Juice of 1 lime
Extra virgin olive oil

SALAD
Safflower or canola oil, for frying the tortillas (see "Shortcut," opposite)

Two 6-inch corn tortillas, cut into strips (more, if you like, or see "Shortcut," opposite)
Juice of 2 limes
1 small jalapeño, halved, seeded, and cut into small dice
Handful of fresh cilantro leaves, chopped
2 teaspoons honey
⅓ cup extra virgin olive oil
6 cups packed mixed greens
1 cup canned black beans, rinsed and drained
½ pint grape tomatoes, halved
Sea salt
1 avocado, pitted, peeled, and cut into ½-inch dice

1. Make the carnitas: Combine the salt, cumin, coriander, and oregano in a small bowl and stir to blend. Rub the spice mixture all over the pork shoulder.
2. Combine the pork, onion, garlic, orange juice, and lime juice in a slow cooker. Cook on high for 4 to 5 hours or low for 8 hours, until the pork is very tender and shreds easily when pierced with a fork. Break up the pork into bite-size chunks. Using two forks, shred the pork.
3. Heat a large skillet over medium-high heat. Add a swirl of olive oil to coat the bottom of the pan. Working in batches so as not to overcrowd the pan, cook the pork until it becomes nicely browned, stirring minimally to get a good crisp going. Getting the pork nice and crispy is a signature step in making carnitas.

4. Line a plate with paper towels. Heat ¼ inch of safflower oil in a small skillet over medium-high heat. Add the tortilla strips and fry until golden and crisp, turning once, 30 to 60 seconds total. Transfer to the paper towel–lined plate to drain.

5. Make the salad: In a deep serving bowl, combine the lime juice, jalapeño, cilantro, and honey. Slowly whisk in the olive oil. Add the mixed greens, black beans, and tomatoes, season with salt, and toss to combine.

6. Scatter the avocado, crisped pork, and tortilla strips on top. Serve immediately.

SHORTCUT

If you don't have time to fry up your own tortillas, buy some good-quality tortilla chips and crumble 1 cup of them onto the salad.

Sides and Veggies

I live with five guys, and they like their meat. But it's important to make meals well rounded, with good-quality vegetables, starches, and other side dishes. So welcome to quinoa, stuffed peppers, and yes, even some kale. It's not the seventies anymore!

Kale and Wild Rice–Stuffed Winter Squash

This is a tasty dish. Between the kale, the rice, and the squash, it's chock-full of fiber, antioxidants, and minerals. And the nutty, salty Pecorino Romano cheese gives it a quiet punch. This makes for a hefty side, and if you add shredded chicken to the stuffing, it becomes a light entrée. ***Makes 4 servings***

Extra virgin olive oil
2 acorn squash, cut in half and seeded
Sea salt and freshly ground black pepper
1 cup wild rice
1 shallot, chopped fine
6 Tuscan kale leaves, ribs removed and leaves chopped fine

1 teaspoon Dijon mustard
Zest of 1 lemon
Handful of fresh flat-leaf parsley leaves, chopped
¼ cup toasted walnuts, chopped (see "Toasting Nuts," page 43)
2 tablespoons grated Pecorino Romano

1. Preheat the oven to 400°F.
2. Rub a bit of oil inside the squash and season with salt and pepper. Place the acorn squash cut sides down on a baking sheet. Bake until tender, 35 to 40 minutes.
3. In a medium saucepan, combine the rice, 1¾ cups of water, and ½ teaspoon of salt. Bring to a boil over medium-high heat, then cover, reduce the heat to low, and cook until the liquid is absorbed, about 40 minutes.
4. Swirl a bit of oil in a medium skillet and heat it over medium heat until shimmering. Add the shallot and sauté until softened, 1 to 2 minutes. Add the kale and sauté just until the leaves begin to wilt, 2 to 3 minutes. Season with salt and pepper. Add the cooked rice, Dijon, and lemon zest and stir to mix well. Cook for 2 minutes more, adding some oil if the rice seems too dry. Stir in the parsley, walnuts, and Pecorino Romano.
5. Remove the squash from the oven. Spoon the rice filling into each half and serve hot.

Warm Quinoa, Shiitake, and Feta Salad

I was eating quinoa long before I knew how to pronounce it correctly (*keen-wah*, by the way). It's one of the upsides to living in a place like L.A., where you're exposed to all sorts of cool things before they're well known, and your family back home thinks you've gone off the deep end because you're eating some weird ancient Peruvian grain.

Quinoa—which grows well at high altitudes—has been the staple food of people living in and around the Andes Mountains of South America for millennia. In the last twenty years, it's made the journey to North America, where it's become quite popular, which is good: it's gluten-free, high in fiber, and contains plenty of protein, iron, and other nutrients.

In terms of cooking, quinoa is very easy to prepare, and goes wonderfully with all sorts flavors, without losing its own distinct taste. Quinoa is a great base for a really healthy, well-rounded meal.

Makes 4 servings

1 cup uncooked quinoa
1½ cups vegetable or chicken broth
Sea salt
2 tablespoons extra virgin olive oil,
    plus more for the mushrooms
6 ounces shiitake mushrooms, stems
    discarded, caps thinly sliced

Freshly ground black pepper
Handful of fresh flat-leaf parsley
    leaves or mint, chopped
Zest and juice of 1 lemon
2 ounces feta cheese, crumbled

1. Combine the quinoa, broth, and a pinch of salt in a small saucepan over medium-high heat. Bring to a boil, cover, and reduce the heat to low. Cook for 10 minutes. Remove from the heat and place a clean kitchen towel between the lid and pot. This helps to absorb condensation and saves you from soggy quinoa. Set the pan aside while you prepare the mushrooms.

2. Heat a medium skillet over medium-high heat. Swirl in a bit of oil to coat the bottom of the pan. Add the mushrooms and season with salt and pepper. Sauté until golden and tender, 3 to 5 minutes.

3. Fluff the quinoa with a fork and transfer to a medium bowl. Add the mushrooms, parsley, lemon zest and juice, and 2 tablespoons olive oil. Mix well, season with salt and pepper, and stir in the feta cheese. The salad may be served warm, at room temperature, or cold.

MAKE IT FANCY

Try topping this dish with a drizzle of truffle oil to take it up a fancy notch.

Cold Sesame Noodles with Cucumber

Remember those sesame noodles I used to order in New York as a cash-strapped actress? Well, I've re-created my own recipe here and, in my humble opinion, it's even better than the original. Best part? This is a cinch to make. **Makes 4 servings**

8 ounces Chinese egg noodles, cappellini, or pad thai–style rice noodles
1 tablespoon peanut oil
¼ cup peanut butter
½ teaspoon toasted sesame oil
3 tablespoons rice vinegar
¼ cup soy sauce
2 teaspoons toasted sesame seeds
1 tablespoon honey
2 tablespoons freshly grated ginger, or 1 tablespoon ground ginger
2 garlic cloves, minced
1 tablespoon red pepper flakes
1 tablespoon sriracha or other red chile sauce
2 Persian cucumbers, 1 grated, 1 thinly sliced
1 scallion, chopped
¼ cup salted roasted peanuts, chopped
¼ cup fresh cilantro leaves, chopped

1. Bring a pot of water to a boil. Prepare a bowl of ice water.
2. Cook the noodles in boiling water until al dente, 3 to 5 minutes. Drain and transfer to a bowl of ice water and soak for 5 minutes, until well chilled. Drain again, return to the bowl, toss with the peanut oil, and set aside.
3. In a large bowl, whisk together the peanut butter, sesame oil, rice vinegar, soy sauce, sesame seeds, honey, ginger, garlic, red pepper flakes, and sriracha. Fold in the grated cucumber, half the scallion, and half the peanuts. Add the chilled pasta and toss to coat thoroughly. Transfer to a serving bowl, twirling the pasta into a nest shape. Top with the sliced cucumber, cilantro, and the remaining scallion and peanuts.

MAKE IT FANCY

Break out the chopsticks and serve your guests the sesame noodles in Chinese takeout boxes—if you ask nicely, your local Chinese restaurant might give you some for free (hey, it's worked for me!). Otherwise, you can buy them really cheap online or at some paper supply stores. Go the extra mile by cutting ¼-inch slices of carrot and using a decorative flower-shaped vegetable cutter to cut out orange flowers to serve on top of the noodles.

Winter Corn Chowder

I am a big fan of creamy soups, and this chowder combines corn, potatoes, and onion to make a nice, creamy broth. Mmm. Add a few Rosemary Oyster Crackers (page 143), and the whole family slows down and relaxes when this gets served.

You'll notice that I use frozen corn for this so I can make it in the winter. Sure, fresh corn is best—there's nothing like it in the summer—but my Midwestern upbringing will not permit me to be a snob about frozen vegetables. These days, you can find very good organic veggies in the freezer section for throwing into recipes here and there.

Makes 4 to 6 servings

4 slices thick-cut bacon, cut into ½-inch pieces
1 small yellow onion, chopped fine
1 (16-ounce) bag frozen corn
Sea salt and freshly ground black pepper

1 russet potato, peeled and cut into ½-inch dice
4 cups vegetable broth
Heavy cream, to serve
1 tablespoon fresh chopped flat-leaf parsley

1. Line a dish with paper towels. Heat a medium saucepan over medium-high heat. Add the bacon and cook until crispy. Use a slotted spoon to transfer to the paper towel–lined dish.

2. Add the onion to the saucepan and sauté until fragrant and softened, 2 to 3 minutes. Add the corn, season with salt and pepper, and sauté 2 minutes, until softened.

3. Add the potato and broth. Increase heat to high, and bring to a boil. Reduce heat to low and simmer until the potato is tender when pierced with a fork, about 15 minutes.

4. Spoon half of the soup into a blender and pulse until smooth. Stir the puree back into the saucepan with the remaining soup. Ladle the soup into bowls and swirl a bit of cream on top of each. Sprinkle the parsley and reserved bacon over the soup. Serve hot with Rosemary Oyster Crackers (opposite), if desired.

See the photo on pages 144-45.

Rosemary Oyster Crackers

I encourage you to make your own crackers *if* you have the time and are feeling ambitious. I quite enjoy making these little crackers, focusing so completely on something for a while, and getting a hundred and fifty tasty prizes for my effort. Plus, they're good on just about any soup, and they can show up on your Glorious Cheese Board (page 79).

Makes about 150 bite-size crackers

1 cup all-purpose flour, plus more
   for dusting
1 teaspoon fine sea salt
1 teaspoon sugar
1 teaspoon baking powder

½ teaspoon finely chopped
   fresh rosemary
2 tablespoons unsalted butter,
   cut into 8 pieces

1. Preheat the oven to 375°F. Line an 11 × 17-inch baking sheet with parchment paper.
2. Combine the flour, salt, sugar, baking powder, and rosemary in a food processor and pulse a few times to blend. Add the butter and pulse about 10 times, until the flour resembles a coarse meal. Add ⅓ cup of cold water and pulse until it forms a craggy-looking dough.
3. Lightly flour a counter or cutting board. Scrape the dough onto the counter and knead a few times until smooth. Cover with a clean kitchen towel and let rest for 15 minutes.
4. On the same surface, roll the dough into a ⅛-inch-thick sheet. Cut the dough into circles using a ¾-inch fluted cutter. You can reroll the scraps once. Place the cutouts on the prepared baking sheet.
5. Bake until the crackers are barely golden around the edges, about 15 minutes. Set aside to cool completely. Store the crackers in an airtight container for up to 1 week.

See the photo on the next page.

Winter Corn Chowder and
Rosemary Oyster Crackers,
pages 142 and 143

Grilled Romaine Hearts with Scallion Cream

I'm new to the grilled lettuce fad, but I like it. I find that a little charring adds a lot of flavor. This recipe is easy and addictive and will make you look like a total gourmet. The scallion cream is tangy and fun, with a nice bite.

Makes 4 servings

4 romaine hearts, cut in half
Extra virgin olive oil
¼ cup heavy cream
2 tablespoons apple cider vinegar
1 teaspoon Dijon mustard

1 teaspoon freshly squeezed
   lemon juice
Sea salt and freshly ground
   black pepper
3 scallions, chopped (white
   and light green parts)

1. Preheat a gas grill to medium-high, or light a charcoal grill.
2. Brush the cut sides of the romaine lightly with oil. Place on the grill (directly over the flame or hot coals) cut sides down and cook until lightly charred, 3 to 5 minutes.
3. Combine the cream, vinegar, mustard, and lemon juice in a small bowl. Season with salt and pepper and whisk to blend. Stir in the scallions.
4. Arrange the romaine hearts on a platter. Spoon the dressing over them and serve immediately.

Roasted Squash and Ginger Soup

Living in California, I've learned how to really love vegetables, including winter squash. Sweet, soothing, and really healthy, it's become one of my favorite foods. Roasting brings out the squash's sweetness, while the ginger offers a quiet zap of pungency. I decided to take a helpful shortcut with this recipe and use precut squash from the produce aisle. It's a nice timesaver, and leaves the recipe open to whatever squash you find available at your local market.

Makes 4 servings

1½ pounds cut-up squash, such as butternut, pumpkin, or acorn
1 shallot, sliced into thin rings
3 tablespoons extra virgin olive oil
Sea salt and freshly ground black pepper

One 1-inch piece of fresh ginger, peeled and thinly sliced
Zest of 1 orange, plus more for garnish
3 cups vegetable or chicken broth, plus more as needed

1. Preheat the oven to 375°F.
2. Combine the squash, shallot, olive oil, and salt and pepper in a 9 × 13-inch roasting pan. Bake for 30 minutes, until very tender when pierced with a fork. Let cool for 5 minutes.
3. Combine the squash mixture, ginger, zest, and broth in a blender (work in batches as needed). Pulse a few times to break up any large pieces of squash, then blend until smooth.
4. Pour the soup into a medium saucepan and cook over medium-low heat until the soup is hot, about 5 minutes. Stir in more broth, ¼ cup at a time, until you reach the desired consistency. Season with salt and pepper if needed.
5. Ladle into bowls and garnish with orange zest and a drizzle of olive oil. Serve hot.

MAKE IT FANCY

Try serving this soup in shot glasses for cocktail parties—just be sure to serve it warm, not blazing hot.

Mozzarella and Sun-Dried Tomato–Stuffed Peppers

I am a great appreciator of sun-dried tomatoes for their sweetness and chewiness. Between the peppers, mozzarella, tomatoes, and herbs, this recipe makes a very tasty side dish. You'll love it. *Makes 4 servings*

Extra virgin olive oil
1 shallot, chopped fine
1 garlic clove, chopped
One (14.5-ounce) can diced tomatoes
½ cup oil-packed sun-dried tomatoes, chopped
½ teaspoon dried basil

½ teaspoon dried oregano
Sea salt and freshly ground black pepper
2 cups cooked rice
1 cup mozzarella, grated
4 red bell peppers

1. Swirl enough oil into a medium skillet to coat the bottom. Heat over medium heat until shimmering. Add the shallot and sauté for 2 minutes, until softened and golden. Add the garlic and sauté for 1 minute.

2. Stir in the diced tomatoes, sun-dried tomatoes, basil, and oregano. Season with salt and pepper. Reduce the heat to low and simmer for 5 minutes.

3. Preheat the oven to 375°F.

4. Remove the sauce from the heat and stir in the rice and ½ cup mozzarella. Set aside.

5. Slice the tops off the bell peppers and scoop out the seeds. Evenly spoon the rice filling into the peppers. Arrange the peppers in an 8-inch square baking dish and sprinkle the remaining ½ cup mozzarella on top.

6. Bake for 35 to 40 minutes, until the peppers are soft and the cheese is lightly golden. Serve hot.

Provençale Casserole

This is a fantastic dish, especially for vegetarian family members or friends—and there are quite a few these days. It's got the ingredients of ratatouille, but is layered, like lasagna.

Makes 6 servings

2 red bell peppers
Extra virgin olive oil
1 leek, thinly sliced (white and light green parts only)
Sea salt and freshly ground black pepper
12 plum tomatoes, cut into ½-inch dice
2 garlic cloves, minced
1 cup vegetable broth
2 teaspoons dried basil, or a handful of fresh basil leaves, chopped

Handful of fresh flat-leaf parsley leaves
Cooking spray
1 medium eggplant (about 12 ounces), cut into ¼-inch-thick rounds
2 zucchini, cut into ¼-inch-thick rounds
1 cup grated Gruyère cheese

1. If you have a gas cooktop, place the peppers directly on a burner over medium heat, turning until they're blackened all over (see "Roasting Peppers," opposite, if you don't have a gas stove). Place the peppers in zip-top bags, close, and let them rest for 5 minutes for the skin to soften. Holding the peppers in a bowl of water, peel the skins off. Discard the skins. Slice the peppers open, remove the seeds, and finely chop the roasted flesh.

2. Swirl a bit of oil in a medium saucepan and heat it over medium-low heat until shimmering. Add the leeks and season with salt and pepper. Cook for 5 minutes, until softened. Add the tomatoes and garlic and sauté until the tomatoes start to soften and break down a bit, 2 to 3 minutes. Stir in the roasted peppers and broth and season with salt and pepper. Increase the heat to medium and bring the mixture to a boil. Turn the heat to low and simmer 10 minutes, until the sauce thickens slightly. Stir in the basil and parsley.

3. Preheat the oven to 375°F. Line a baking sheet with foil or parchment paper.

1. Coat a 9-inch deep-dish pie plate with cooking spray. Spread one quarter of the sauce on the bottom of the dish. Alternate slices of eggplant and zucchini in a circle to make a layer covering the bottom of the pie plate. Spoon another quarter of the sauce on over the vegetables. Cover with a handful of grated cheese. Repeat with another layer of the eggplant and zucchini and top with half of the remaining sauce and cheese. Repeat with the remaining eggplant, zucchini, sauce, and cheese. Drizzle with olive oil. Season with salt and pepper.
5. Place the casserole onto the prepared baking sheet. Bake until the sauce is bubbling, the vegetables are tender, and the cheese is melted and golden brown, 50 to 60 minutes.

ROASTING PEPPERS

Peppers can also be roasted on an outdoor grill, or using the broiler setting on your oven. Jarred, store-bought roasted peppers can be swapped in, too.

Flatbread Caprese

I don't consider myself a baker, but I do enjoy baking shows like *The Great British Bake-Off*. And sometimes on a rainy afternoon, I get inspired to have some fun and try something new. This is my attempt at a homemade flatbread . . . it turned out surprisingly well!

Makes 4 appetizer servings or 2 main-course servings

2 cups all-purpose flour, plus
    more for kneading
½ teaspoon active dry yeast
1 teaspoon sea salt, plus more
    as needed
¼ teaspoon sugar
1 cup warm water (105°F to 110°F,
    or see "No Thermometer?,"
    page 70)

Extra virgin olive oil
4 ounces fresh mozzarella, cut
    into ½-inch cubes
½ pint grape tomatoes, sliced
    into ¼-inch-thick rounds
Handful of fresh basil leaves

1. Combine the flour, yeast, salt, and sugar in a large bowl and whisk to blend. Stir in the water until it forms a rough dough.

2. Sprinkle some flour on a counter or cutting board. Turn the dough out onto the board and sprinkle a bit more flour on top. Knead until the dough becomes a smooth ball, 3 to 4 minutes, adding more flour as needed. Cover the dough with a clean kitchen towel and let it rest on the counter for 10 minutes.

3. Preheat the oven to 425°F. Coat a baking sheet with cooking spray.

4. Roll the dough into a 9 × 17-inch rectangle and transfer it to the prepared pan. Drizzle with a bit of olive oil and bake 18 to 20 minutes, until golden and crisp.

5. Meanwhile, combine the mozzarella and tomatoes in a medium bowl. Slice the basil into ribbons and add them to the bowl, along with a drizzle of oil. Season with salt.

6. Transfer the flatbread to a cutting board. Scatter the mozzarella mixture on top. Cut the flatbread lengthwise, then into triangles. Serve immediately.

Fried Rice

Although I ordered plenty of fried rice from my local Chinese restaurant back in the day, I prefer making my own because I find that the fresh ingredients really make a difference. Plus, many restaurants put too much salt, or even MSG, into their food—both of which I try to avoid when cooking for my family. Feel free to experiment with any type of meat (I use pork here), tofu, or bean; they're all delicious. This recipe is great to serve at a family meal, an intimate party, or the next time you binge-watch TV all weekend.

Makes 4 servings

2 eggs
Sea salt and freshly ground black
  pepper
Canola or olive oil
2 boneless center-cut pork chops,
  diced
1 tablespoon sesame oil
1 small yellow onion, chopped
1 teaspoon freshly grated ginger

3 cups cold, cooked white rice
3 tablespoons soy sauce, plus more
  to taste
1 cup frozen peas and carrots,
  thawed
1 red Fresno chile, halved, seeded,
  and thinly sliced, optional
2 to 3 scallions, chopped

1. Crack the eggs into a small bowl, season them with salt and pepper, and beat them lightly with a fork.
2. Heat a deep skillet over medium-high heat. Swirl in enough oil to coat the bottom of the pan. Add the eggs, and cook, stirring a few times, until cooked through. Transfer the eggs to a medium bowl.
3. Turn the heat to high and add another swirl of oil if the pan seems too dry. Add the pork and sauté until golden and cooked through, 2 to 3 minutes. Transfer to the bowl with the eggs.
4. In the same skillet, heat the sesame oil over medium-high heat. Add the onion and sauté until softened, about 1 minute. Add the ginger and rice, making sure to break up any clumps of rice. Stir in the soy sauce, peas and carrots, pork and eggs, and chile, if using. Sauté until the rice is heated through. Season with salt, or add more soy sauce, to taste.
5. Spoon the rice into a deep bowl or platter. Garnish with the scallions before serving.

Classic Mac 'n' Cheese

I don't eat mac 'n' cheese too much because I like to watch my waistline, but when I really want to indulge—and promise to go to the gym the next day—I'll have some. It's always worth it.

You'll notice that I use American cheese in this recipe, which you can get in slices or in a block from the deli section of the grocery store. It melts easily and mimics best what we ate out of the box back in Cleveland. This was a standard dish in our home when the boys were younger.

Makes 6 to 8 servings

1 pound uncooked elbow pasta
8 ounces American cheese slices, torn into pieces or crumbled
¾ cup grated Pecorino Romano
1 cup 2% or whole milk

2 tablespoons unsalted butter
¼ teaspoon paprika
Pinch of dry mustard
Sea salt

1. Bring a large pot of water to a boil. Cook the pasta al dente, according to the package directions.
2. Meanwhile, combine the cheeses, milk, butter, paprika, and mustard in a large pot over medium-low heat. Cook, stirring occasionally, until the cheese and butter are completely melted, 5 to 7 minutes.
3. Drain the pasta. Add it to the pot with the cheese sauce and season with salt. Stir to coat the pasta, then cook for 2 minutes more. Serve hot.

Sweet Things

Sweet things make people happy. It's a law of the universe.

In this section, I cover ice cream, puddings, cookies, tarts, tartlets, Pop-Tarts, and, oh . . . five types of cake. And if that's not enough for you, there are even more sweet things in the Guest Goodies chapter.

You're welcome.

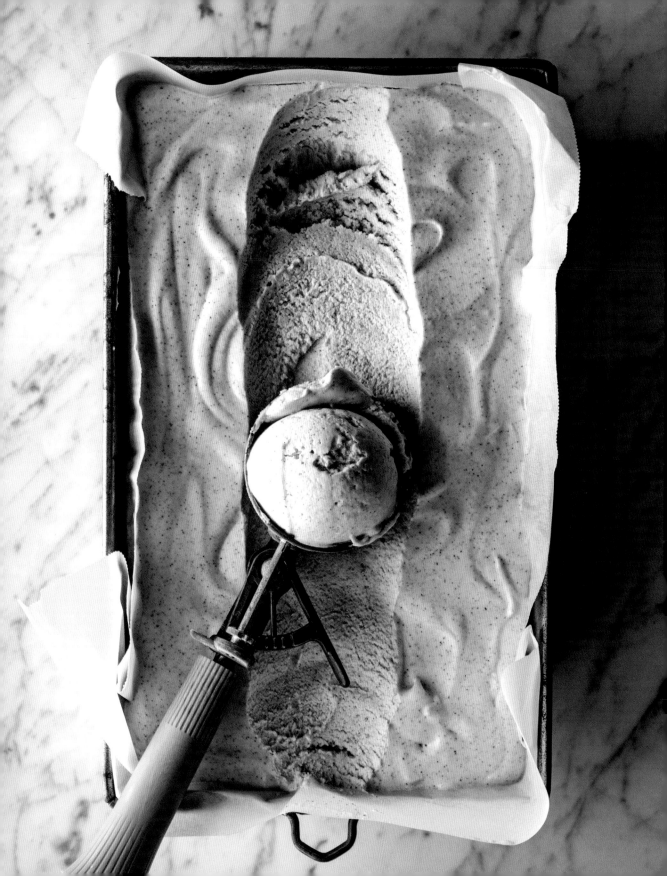

No-Churn Pumpkin Spice Ice Cream

I don't know when pumpkin took over the culinary world, but it's here to stay, and not just at Starbucks. Lucky for me, it's one of my favorite things. I love pumpkin-stuffed pasta and pumpkin pie, so when I discovered pumpkin-flavored ice cream? I declared a national holiday in Patty World.

This recipe makes an ice cream with a lovely, soft consistency, but if you want to give it a more dynamic texture or taste, consider adding fun things like chopped pistachios, chopped figs, or crumbled bits of ginger snaps. **Makes about 3 pints**

One 14-ounce can sweetened
   condensed milk
Seeds of 1 vanilla bean, scraped out, or
   1 teaspoon pure vanilla extract

1 teaspoon ground cinnamon
½ teaspoon ground ginger
¼ teaspoon ground cloves
2 cups heavy cream

1. Line each of two 8-inch loaf pans with a sheet of waxed paper long enough to hang over the long sides.
2. Pour the milk into a large bowl. Add the vanilla bean seeds, cinnamon, ginger, and cloves. Whisk to blend.
3. Beat the cream in a separate large bowl until stiff peaks form. Scoop one third of the whipped cream into the condensed milk mixture and stir to loosen the mixture. Add the remaining whipped cream and fold it in with a rubber spatula. You'll lose less volume this way.
4. Evenly divide the mixture between the prepared pans. Cover with more parchment paper and freeze until firm enough to scoop, about 6 hours. The ice cream will keep in the freezer, wrapped tightly, for up to 1 week.

Raspberry Yogurt Ice Pops

Got kids hanging around in the summer? These pops make a refreshing treat, and once you've made them, they're ready in the freezer anytime your kids' friends just show up. Which they will. I also like these pops because they don't contain the preservatives and artificial coloring that you'll find in most store-bought ice pops. **Makes 6 servings**

1½ cups plain yogurt
1½ cups frozen raspberries (or any
    frozen fruit you like)

¼ cup pure maple syrup
1½ tablespoons freshly squeezed
    lemon juice

1. Combine all the ingredients in a blender and blend until smooth.
2. Pour into ice pop molds. Freeze at least 6 hours or overnight.
3. To serve, run the frozen pops (still in the molds) under a little hot water to loosen them.

MAKE IT FANCY

Try adding dried bits of edible lavender or fresh lemon thyme leaves.

MAKE IT FANCY

These tartlets are tasty as is, but if you want to further impress with minimal extra effort, top the curd with berries—blueberries or blackberries would be yummy, but use whatever you're in the mood for—and dust some confectioners' sugar over them. Alternatively, you could top them with some slivered mint or even some edible flower petals.

Lemon-Orange Curd Tartlets

"Curd" sounds so British, doesn't it? Across the pond, Brits like to eat citrus curd with scones, while I prefer to slather mine on toast at breakfast. But curd is also amazing as a dessert filling, so I fill mini prebaked phyllo shells with curd for a handheld dessert at parties, and they always elicit oohs and ahhs.

Makes 48 tartlets, which will serve about 12

4 large egg yolks
6 tablespoons sugar
¼ cup freshly squeezed lemon juice
3 tablespoons freshly squeezed
   orange juice

1 teaspoon grated lemon zest
½ teaspoon grated orange zest
3 tablespoons cold unsalted butter,
   cut into six 1-inch pieces
48 store-bought phyllo cups, thawed

1. Pour enough water into a medium saucepan to come about 1 inch up the sides. Bring to a simmer over medium-low heat.

2. Meanwhile, in a medium stainless steel or glass heatproof bowl that will nestle in the saucepan without touching the water, whisk the egg yolks and sugar for 1 minute. Place the bowl just inside the rim of the saucepan, reducing the heat as necessary so that the water does not boil. Add the lemon and orange juices and zests and whisk to combine. Cook slowly, whisking constantly to prevent the lemon mixture from sticking to the bottom and sides of the pan, until thick enough to coat the back of a spoon, 9 to 12 minutes.

3. Remove from the heat. Immediately stir in one piece of butter at a time, using a flat rubber spatula to incorporate, until the curd is thick, smooth, and completely cool.

4. Strain the curd into a clean container, pressing down on the strainer with the spatula to extract as much as possible. Discard the solids left in the strainer.

5. Fill each phyllo cup with 3 teaspoons of curd and serve within 2 or 3 hours. If you have any curd left, refrigerate in a tightly sealed container and eat within 1 week.

Chocolate Chile Tart

This is a fun and modern take on the chocolate pie I knew as a kid. You can make this tart up to two days ahead, if that makes your life easier. You'll love it. **_Makes 8 servings_**

CRUST

1¼ cups all-purpose flour, plus
    extra for rolling the dough
3 tablespoons cocoa powder
1 teaspoon instant espresso
    granules, optional
3 teaspoons sugar
¼ teaspoon sea salt
8 tablespoons (1 stick) very cold
    butter, cut into 16 pieces

FILLING

1½ cups heavy cream
⅔ cup sugar
1 teaspoon cayenne
One 10-ounce bag bittersweet
    (52%) chocolate chips

Whipped cream to serve,
    optional

1. Preheat the oven to 425°F.
2. Make the crust: Combine the flour, cocoa powder, espresso (if using), sugar, and salt in a food processor. Pulse once or twice to mix well. Add the butter and pulse a few more times, until it forms a sandy-looking mixture, 4 or 5 one-second pulses. Add 6 to 8 tablespoons ice cold water, 1 tablespoon at a time, pulsing after each addition, until the dough begins to clump together, 30 to 60 seconds.
3. Scoop the dough out onto a clean, flat work surface dusted with flour. Knead gently a few times to form a smooth ball. Roll out the dough into a circle large enough to fit a 9-inch tart pan. Press the crust into the pan. Place a sheet of parchment over the crust and fill it with uncooked rice, dried beans, or pie weights. Bake 10 to 12 minutes, until the crust is fragrant (it's hard to get a visual cue from a chocolate crust) and pulls away slightly from the sides of the pan. Remove the parchment and pie weights. Let the pie crust cool completely before moving on to next step.
4. Make the filling: Combine the cream, sugar, and cayenne in a small saucepan over medium-low heat. Cook until the cream is hot but not boiling, and the sugar is completely dissolved.
5. Place the chips in a medium bowl and pour the hot cream mixture on top. Let sit for 2 minutes, then stir until the chocolate is completely melted.
6. Pour the filling into the baked tart shell. Chill until firm, at least 4 hours and preferably overnight. Serve slices with whipped cream, if desired.

Coconut-Lime Rice Pudding with Praline Pistachios

Full disclosure: I don't like rice pudding very much. But Dave adores it, so in the name of harmonious, long-term matrimony, I've learned how to make it. And over the years, I've snuck in all the things I love—coconut, lime, pistachios—so when I sneak a taste of his, it's not so bad! He raves about this recipe.

Makes 8 servings

4 cups cold cooked white rice
4 cups canned coconut milk (this is almost 2½ 13.5-ounce cans), well shaken

⅔ to 1 cup plus 2 teaspoons sugar, depending on your sweetness preference
Zest of 2 limes
½ cup raw, unsalted shelled pistachios

1. Combine the rice, coconut milk, ⅔ cup sugar, and the lime zest in a large saucepan over medium-high heat. Just before it reaches a full boil, reduce the heat to low. Taste to see if the sweetness is to your liking, and add more sugar if desired. Let the rice mixture simmer, stirring occasionally, until slightly thickened, 8 to 10 minutes. It'll continue to thicken as it cools.
2. Meanwhile, place the pistachios in a small nonstick skillet over medium-high heat. Cook, shaking the pan occasionally, until the nuts are lightly golden and fragrant, 2 to 3 minutes.
3. Add 2 teaspoons sugar to the skillet. Let the pan sit undisturbed for 30 seconds, until the sugar begins to melt. Add a few drops of water—it'll sizzle and steam up immediately. Shake the pan until the pistachios are coated all around (they'll look crystallized). Let cool a few minutes before using. (These may be prepared up to 2 days in advance and stored in a covered container at room temperature until ready to use.)
4. You can serve the rice pudding warm. To serve it cold, transfer it to a container and chill for at least 2 hours, and up to 3 days (it'll thicken significantly when refrigerated, so you can stir in some extra coconut milk or water to thin it out to desired consistency, if you like). Spoon into bowls and sprinkle some of the candied pistachios on top just before serving.

Bourbon Pecan–Glazed Pound Cake

Despite my sister throwing an entire pound cake at my head when I was ten, I still love them, and adding bourbon just eases the pain of that childhood memory.

And let's be honest: You can't beat homemade baked goods; there's a difference when all the ingredients are fresh, and there are no preservatives. It's worth taking the time to bake for your friends and family.

FYI: This cake is well served by a day's rest (the glaze benefits, too, because the bourbon flavor softens a bit). It allows the crumb time to settle and compact into itself, giving it that hefty texture you expect from a pound cake. Properly wrapped—in parchment paper, *not* foil or plastic wrap—it'll keep for up to three days. **Makes 8 servings**

CAKE
½ pound (2 sticks) unsalted
   butter, softened
1 cup sugar
1 teaspoon pure vanilla extract
3 large eggs, at room temperature
2 cups all-purpose flour
1 teaspoon baking powder
½ teaspoon sea salt
¼ cup buttermilk

GLAZE
1 cup confectioners' sugar, sifted
1 tablespoon freshly squeezed
   orange juice
1 tablespoon butter, melted
1 tablespoon bourbon (or 1 extra
   tablespoon orange juice)
¼ cup pecans, toasted and chopped
   (see "Toasting Nuts," page 43)

1. Preheat the oven to 325°F. Line a 9-inch loaf pan with a sheet of parchment paper long enough to hang over the longer sides of the pan. The paper will act as a sling to easily lift the cake from the pan.

2. Make the cake: Combine the butter and granulated sugar in a large bowl. Beat with an electric mixer until fluffy and well mixed. Add the vanilla and the eggs, one at a time, beating after each addition until the batter is light and fluffy.

3. Add the flour, baking powder, and salt. Beat until just mixed, with no visible signs of flour. Add the buttermilk and beat again until just mixed; 15 to 30 seconds should do it.

4. Scrape the batter into the prepared loaf pan and bake 70 to 75 minutes, until deep golden on top and a metal skewer inserted comes out clean. Set the cake pan on a wire rack to cool completely.

5. Make the glaze when the cake is cool. In a small bowl, combine the confectioners' sugar, juice, butter, and bourbon. Whisk until the sugar has completely dissolved and a thick glaze forms.

6. Remove the cake from the pan, and set it directly on the wire rack. Pour the glaze lengthwise down the center of the cake. Spread it to the sides using an offset spatula. Sprinkle the pecans over the glaze. Let the glaze set until it can be tapped without any sticking to your finger, at least 20 minutes.

Earl Grey Flourless Chocolate Cake

Being married to a Brit, I've fallen in love with Earl Grey tea. It's one of the stronger teas, and adding it to this cake gives it that lovely surprise taste, a bit of sophistication and international flair. Personally, I love all things British, so it holds a special place in my heart.

This is the perfect make-ahead recipe. It's tender on day one and settles into a dense, rich cake on days two and three. It's truly the kind of cake that gets better with age.

Makes 8 to 10 servings

Butter or cooking spray, for the pan
10 ounces bittersweet or dark
   chocolate chips
2 Earl Grey teabags

5 large eggs, at room temperature,
   separated
Fleur de sel sea salt
2/3 cup sugar
1 tablespoon almond flour

1. Set an oven rack in the center position and preheat the oven to 350°F.
2. Grease the sides and bottoms of a 9-inch round cake pan. Cut a piece of parchment paper long enough to hang over the edges of the pan. Press it in as best you can; it won't settle perfectly and that's okay. The batter will weigh it down.
3. Set up a double boiler to melt the chocolate (this helps the chocolate infuse with the tea better than melting it in the microwave). Fill a medium saucepan one third of the way up with water. Set it over high heat and place a metal or glass bowl on the saucepan. It should fit snugly but not touch the water. Bring the water to a boil. Add the chocolate and teabags to the bowl and reduce the heat to a simmer. Give the chocolate a stir with a spatula when it begins to melt. Let the melted chocolate steep with the teabags while you continue preparing the batter.
4. Combine the egg whites and a pinch of salt in a clean and dry large bowl. Beat on high speed until they become glossy and stiff peaks form.
5. In a separate clean medium bowl, combine the egg yolks, sugar, and 1/4 teaspoon salt. Beat until the yolks double in volume.

6. Remove the teabags from the chocolate and discard them. Use a wooden spoon or spatula to stir the chocolate into the egg yolk mixture. Add the almond flour and stir until combined (it will be a very thick, stiff batter).

7. Stir in one third of the egg whites to loosen up the batter. Use a rubber spatula to fold in the remaining egg whites.

8. Gently spoon the batter into the prepared pan, taking care that the parchment goes down into the sides of the pan as much as it can. Bake for 25 to 28 minutes, or until the cake puffs up and the top looks dry. Let the cake cool in the pan on a wire rack. The cake will "fall" a little as it cools. When cooled, the cake can be wrapped in parchment paper and stored at room temperature for up to 3 days.

Raspberry-Lemon Icebox Cake

I love gingersnaps. We happily ate them growing up, but Mom never thought to use them in a recipe! This is a pretty, light, and fun dessert, perfect for a summer brunch or ladies' lunch.

Makes 8 servings

2½ cups heavy cream
6 ounces cream cheese, softened
1 cup confectioners' sugar
Zest and juice of 1 lemon

½ pint fresh raspberries
24 packaged gingersnaps

1. In a medium bowl, beat the cream with a hand mixer until soft peaks form. Set aside.
2. In a large bowl, combine the cream cheese and confectioners' sugar with the lemon juice and zest. Beat until creamy and well blended. Add the raspberries and use a rubber spatula to smash and stir them into the cream cheese mixture. Gently fold in the whipped cream.
3. Line a 9 × 3-inch loaf pan with a sheet of parchment paper long enough to hang over the sides (this will act as a sling to lift out the cake when it's ready to serve).
4. Arrange 8 gingersnaps in a single layer in the bottom of the pan. Spread one third of the filling over the cookies. Repeat this process twice with the remaining cookies and cream, making three layers in all.
5. Chill in the fridge for at least 6 hours, and preferably overnight. When ready to serve, lift the cake out of the pan and cut into slices.

Toasted Marshmallow Milk Shake

You heard me: *Marshmallow. Milk shake.*

One day when I was fooling around in the kitchen, I discovered that the Diet Police wouldn't show up at my door when I dunked a crispy, burned marshmallow (I do it on the gas stove) into the blender with some ice cream. I've been whizzing up these babies ever since. They're what I call WTC: Worth the Calories. And when I get caught mallow-handed, I pretend I'm making them for the kids. Slurp.

Makes 4 servings

12 marshmallows, toasted (see Note, below)
1 pint vanilla ice cream
1½ cups 2% or whole milk
Whipped cream, to serve

1. Combine 8 of the marshmallows, the ice cream, and the milk in a blender. Cover and blend until well mixed.
2. Divide the milk shake among four glasses. Garnish each with whipped cream and a marshmallow. Serve immediately.

Note: *You can toast the marshmallows using a few methods. If it's summertime and you have a fire pit, go for it. Otherwise, you can use a burner on a gas stove and toast them over the flame. If you have an electric oven, arrange the marshmallows on a parchment-lined baking sheet and bake them in a preheated 350ºF oven for 10 to 12 minutes, until puffed and golden.*

MAKE IT FANCY

Upgrade your milk shake with a powdered graham cracker rim. Crush 4 graham crackers. Before filling the glasses, dip the rims in a bit of ice cream, then into the crushed graham crackers.

Strawberry Pop-Tarts

We ate Pop-Tarts growing up, but because my mother was a health nut, we weren't allowed to have the ones with the frosting on them! So, in honor of my mom, this is my semi-frosted workaround, and the way to give your kids Pop-Tarts without feeling guilty. Nutella works really well in these pastry tarts, too.

Makes 6 Pop-Tarts

1⅓ cups all-purpose flour, plus more
   for rolling the dough
¼ cup cornstarch
1½ cups confectioners' sugar
Pinch of sea salt
⅛ teaspoon baking soda
¼ teaspoon baking powder

4 tablespoons (½ stick) cold
   unsalted butter, cut into 8 pieces
¼ cup plus 2 tablespoons heavy
   cream
¼ cup Strawberry Jam (page 215)
¼ to ½ teaspoon almond extract
Rainbow sprinkles

1. Preheat the oven to 375°F. Line an 11 × 17-inch baking sheet with parchment paper.
2. Combine the flour, cornstarch, ½ cup of the confectioners' sugar, the salt, baking soda, and baking powder in a food processor and pulse to blend. Add the butter and pulse four or five times, until it forms a sandy-looking mixture with some pebble-size pieces. Pour in the cream. Pulse a few times, then process 30 to 60 seconds, until the dough comes together in a rough ball.
3. Place the dough on a lightly floured counter or cutting board. Gently knead a few times, until it comes together into a smooth ball. Roll the dough out to a 1/16-inch thickness; you should have an 11 × 22-inch rectangle. Trim any rough edges with a knife or pizza cutter (pro tip!). Cut the rectangle into 12 even-size rectangles (about 4½ × 2¾ inches each).
4. Place 6 of the pastry rectangles on the prepared pan. Spoon 2 teaspoons of jam onto each center and spread it out, leaving a ½-inch border. Cover each with one of the remaining plain pastries. Use a fork to crimp the edges closed.
5. Bake 15 to 17 minutes, until crisp and golden around the edges. Transfer to a wire rack to cool completely.
6. In a medium bowl, combine the remaining 1 cup confectioners' sugar with 4 to 6 teaspoons of cold water and the almond extract. Whisk until smooth. Drizzle over the cooled tarts or spread it on with an offset spatula. Decorate with sprinkles.

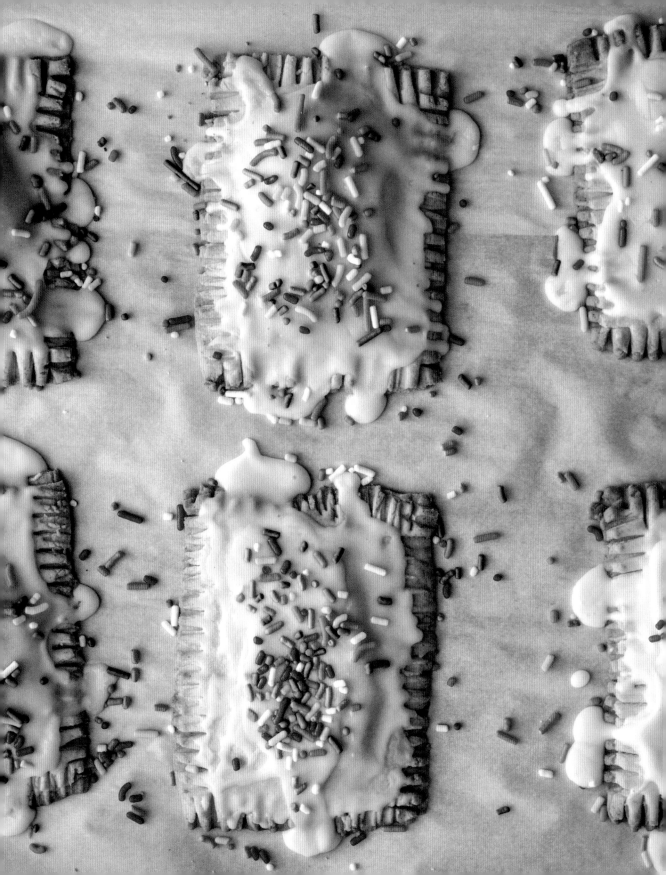

CORNY QUESTION

What's the difference between polenta, grits, and cornmeal? Well, they're all corn products, but polenta (from Italy) and grits (from the American South) come from a coarser grind of corn than cornmeal, which is more like a flour.

Polenta, Pine Nut, and Rosemary Olive Oil Cake

Olive oil cake is a classic dessert all over Italy. Using olive oil (usually extra virgin, for its stronger, sweeter taste) instead of butter or other vegetable oils makes olive oil cake dense and flavorful. In this recipe, I've added some polenta (another Italian staple) to give it a nice, nubbly texture and the mild sweetness of corn. Feel free to experiment with this, adding fresh blueberries or other fruits. It's an elegant choice for friends or family, and goes perfectly after an Italian classic like Eggplant Parmigiana (page 96) or Spaghetti Bolognese (page 98).   ***Makes 10 to 12 servings***

Cooking spray
1¼ cups all-purpose flour, plus
    more for dusting the pan
¾ cup polenta (not instant)
2 teaspoons baking powder
½ teaspoon sea salt
1 tablespoon finely chopped
    fresh rosemary

Zest of 2 lemons
4 large eggs, at room temperature
1 cup sugar
¾ cup extra virgin olive oil
½ cup pine nuts
Confectioners' sugar, optional

1. Preheat the oven to 350°F. Coat the bottom and sides of a 9-inch springform pan with cooking spray. Dust the pan with a bit of flour, tapping out any excess.
2. In a large bowl, combine the flour, polenta, baking powder, salt, rosemary, and lemon zest. Whisk to blend.
3. Combine the eggs and sugar in a separate large bowl. Using a hand mixer, beat until fluffy and tripled in volume, 3 to 5 minutes. Add the flour mixture and oil and stir until just combined, with no visible traces of flour. Scrape the batter into the prepared pan. Evenly sprinkle the pine nuts over the top.
4. Bake until the cake is deep golden and pulls away slightly from the sides of the pan, 30 to 35 minutes. The cake will sink a bit as it cools. Let cool completely. Dust with confectioners' sugar before serving, if desired.

Cherry Cola Sheet Cake

On Friday nights back in Cleveland, we kids would settle in to watch *Jonny Quest* and drink Mom's homemade root beer floats. That was a big treat. So any recipe that includes soda pop—whether it's Coke, cherry cola, or root beer—brings back a lot of memories, but in a new and fun way.

This is a great recipe for making a couple of days ahead of time, as it just improves with age.

Makes 24 servings

CAKE

2½ cups all-purpose flour
1 cup granulated sugar
¼ cup cocoa powder
1 teaspoon baking soda
¼ teaspoon sea salt
One (12-ounce) can cherry cola
1 cup canola, grapeseed, or
  vegetable oil
2 large eggs
½ cup buttermilk, well shaken
1 teaspoon pure vanilla extract

ICING

One (12-ounce) can cherry cola
8 tablespoons (1 stick) cold
  unsalted butter, cut into
  16 pieces
¼ cup unsweetened cocoa
  powder, sifted
3 cups confectioners' sugar,
  sifted

1. Preheat the oven to 350°F. Line a 9 × 13-inch baking sheet with a piece of parchment paper that is long enough to hang over the longer sides.
2. Make the cake: In a large bowl, whisk the flour, granulated sugar, cocoa, baking soda, and salt. Add the cola, oil, eggs, buttermilk, and vanilla and whisk until just combined, with no visible traces of flour.
3. Pour the batter into the prepared pan. Bake for 35 to 40 minutes, until a toothpick inserted in the center comes out clean.
4. Halfway through baking, prepare the icing. In a small saucepan over medium-high heat, simmer the cola until it's reduced to ½ cup, 12 to 15 minutes. Whisk in the butter, a few pieces at a time, until it's completely dissolved. Combine the cocoa and confectioners' sugar, and whisk them in, 1 cup at a time, until the icing is smooth.
5. As soon as the cake comes out of the oven, spread the icing over it. Set the cake on a wire rack and let it cool completely before serving. Wrapped in parchment paper, the cake will stay fresh for up to 3 days.

Spring Cleaning Cookies

Every spring, when shooting season wraps, I do a thorough cleaning of the house to get rid of all the detritus that has accumulated over the previous months. One year I realized I could do the same thing in the kitchen and put lots of odds and ends into a cookie! So whatever you have in the pantry, try it: peanut butter chips, chocolate chips, pumpkin seeds, dried cranberries, potato chip bits, or walnuts—you can even add a few table-spoons of finely ground coffee (unbrewed, not used grounds). What have you got to lose? My one suggestion: As you experiment, try for a balance between sweet and salty.

Makes 20 cookies

8 tablespoons (1 stick) unsalted
   butter, softened
½ cup firmly packed light brown
   sugar
¼ cup granulated sugar
1 large egg, at room temperature

1 teaspoon pure vanilla extract
1¼ cups all-purpose flour
1 teaspoon baking soda
½ teaspoon sea salt
2½ cups mix-ins (see headnote)

1. Preheat the oven to 350°F. Line two baking sheets with parchment paper.
2. In a large bowl, use a hand mixer to beat the butter and sugars until smooth and creamy. Add the egg and vanilla and beat until well blended. Add the flour, baking soda, and salt and beat just until mixed, with no visible signs of flour.
3. Add the mix-ins and stir to combine.
4. Drop the dough by heaping 1½ tablespoons onto the prepared baking sheets, spacing the dough mounds 2 inches apart. Bake, one sheet at a time, until the bottoms and edges of the cookies are lightly browned, 12 to 14 minutes (less time for a super-chewy cookie, more for a crisper cookie). Let the cookies cool on the baking sheets for 5 minutes. Transfer to wire racks to cool completely.

Summer Peach Hand Pies

This recipe is what happens when a peach pie and an empanada have babies. Made with fresh peaches at the peak of summer, these are fantastic for kids to run around the yard with. Feel free to use premade pastry dough if you need to, but I'd keep the peaches fresh.

Makes 8 servings

FILLING

3 ripe peaches, peeled, pitted, and chopped
½ Granny Smith apple, grated (no need to peel)
Zest of 1 lemon
Juice of ½ lemon
½ cup sugar
2 tablespoons all-purpose flour
Pinch of sea salt

PIE CRUST

1¾ cups all-purpose flour, plus more for rolling out the dough
1 teaspoon granulated sugar
½ teaspoon sea salt
8 tablespoons (1 stick) cold unsalted butter, cut into 16 pieces
1½ teaspoons white vinegar
1 large egg

1 egg white, beaten with 1 teaspoon water
Coarse sugar, such as Sugar in the Raw

1. Place an oven rack in the top third of the oven and preheat the oven to 425°F. Line an 11 × 17-inch baking sheet with a piece of parchment paper long enough to extend over all the sides (this makes for quick and easy cleanup).
2. Make the filling: In a medium bowl, combine the peaches, apple, lemon zest, juice, sugar, flour, and salt. Mix well and set aside.
3. Make the pie crust: Add the flour, sugar, and salt to the bowl of a food processor and pulse to blend. Add the butter and pulse a few times, until it forms a sandy-looking mixture with some pebble-size pieces. Add the vinegar, egg, and 3 tablespoons very cold water, 1 tablespoon at a time, pulsing after each addition just until the dough forms a solid ball (this may take up to 1 minute).
4. Lightly flour a countertop or cutting board. Divide the dough into 8 equal-size pieces. Gently roll them into balls and place them on the lightly floured surface.

Flatten the balls slightly into a circle using the palm of your hand. Dust the tops of each with a bit of flour. Using a rolling pin dusted with flour, roll each out into a 6-inch circle, but don't fret if they're not perfectly round. Pie making should be fun, not stressful.

5. Divide the filling evenly among the pastry circles, placing the filling onto one side and leaving a ½-inch border.

6. Fold the unfilled half of dough over the filling on each pie. Press the edges down to seal, forming half-moon shapes. Transfer the pies to the prepared baking sheet and use the tines of a fork to crimp the edges closed. Brush the tops with a bit of the egg wash and sprinkle tops with the coarse sugar. Use a fork to prick a few holes in the tops so the pies don't explode while baking.

7. Bake for 20 minutes, then reduce the oven temperature to 350°F. Bake for 15 to 20 minutes more, until the pies are golden and juices begin to bubble slightly. Let the pies cool at least 15 minutes before serving. When cooled completely, the pies may be stored in an airtight container at room temperature for up to 2 days.

The Happiest Hour

Good drinks can make a party. Of course, we're all supposed *to open up to one another naturally, but it's no secret that a little fermented lubrication helps. With the aid of just an ounce of booze, new relationships start, movie ideas get hatched, and marital tensions are eased. Aren't they, Dave?*

In this chapter, I've got some great ideas for punches, cocktails, hot drinks, and even mocktails for kids and teetotalers. Bottoms up!

Maple-Bourbon Old-Fashioned

I'm a bourbon girl who enjoys a good old-fashioned. And honestly, I love the name as much as the drink; it sounds so forties . . . "I'll have an old-*fashioned*, barkeep!"

    This is my twist, using maple syrup instead of granulated sugar. It makes a subtle, but pleasing, difference.

Makes 2 servings

3 ounces bourbon
1 teaspoon pure maple syrup
Orange bitters

Freshly opened bottle or can of
  seltzer
Two 2-inch strips of lemon peel
2 Luxardo maraschino cherries

1. Fill two rocks glasses with ice.
2. Divide the bourbon and maple syrup between the glasses. Give a few shakes of bitters into each glass, then a few splashes of seltzer.
3. Garnish each cocktail with a strip of lemon peel and a cherry.

Patty's Party Punch

A good punch can make a party. First of all, it frees you up to do other things besides restock the bar, and second, it's a fresh and sneaky way to get everyone tipsy. This punch can be made through step 2 up to one day in advance.

Makes 18 servings, or roughly 3 quarts

4 cups (1 quart) cranberry juice
4 cups (1 quart) freshly squeezed
   orange juice
2½ cups bourbon or rum

Two 12-ounce bottles ginger beer
Few dashes of orange bitters
½ cup frozen cranberries
1 thinly sliced orange, for garnish

1. Pour the cranberry juice, orange juice, and bourbon into a punch bowl and stir to combine.
2. Add the ginger beer and add a few shakes of orange bitters. Stir to mix.
3. Add the frozen cranberries and sliced orange before serving.

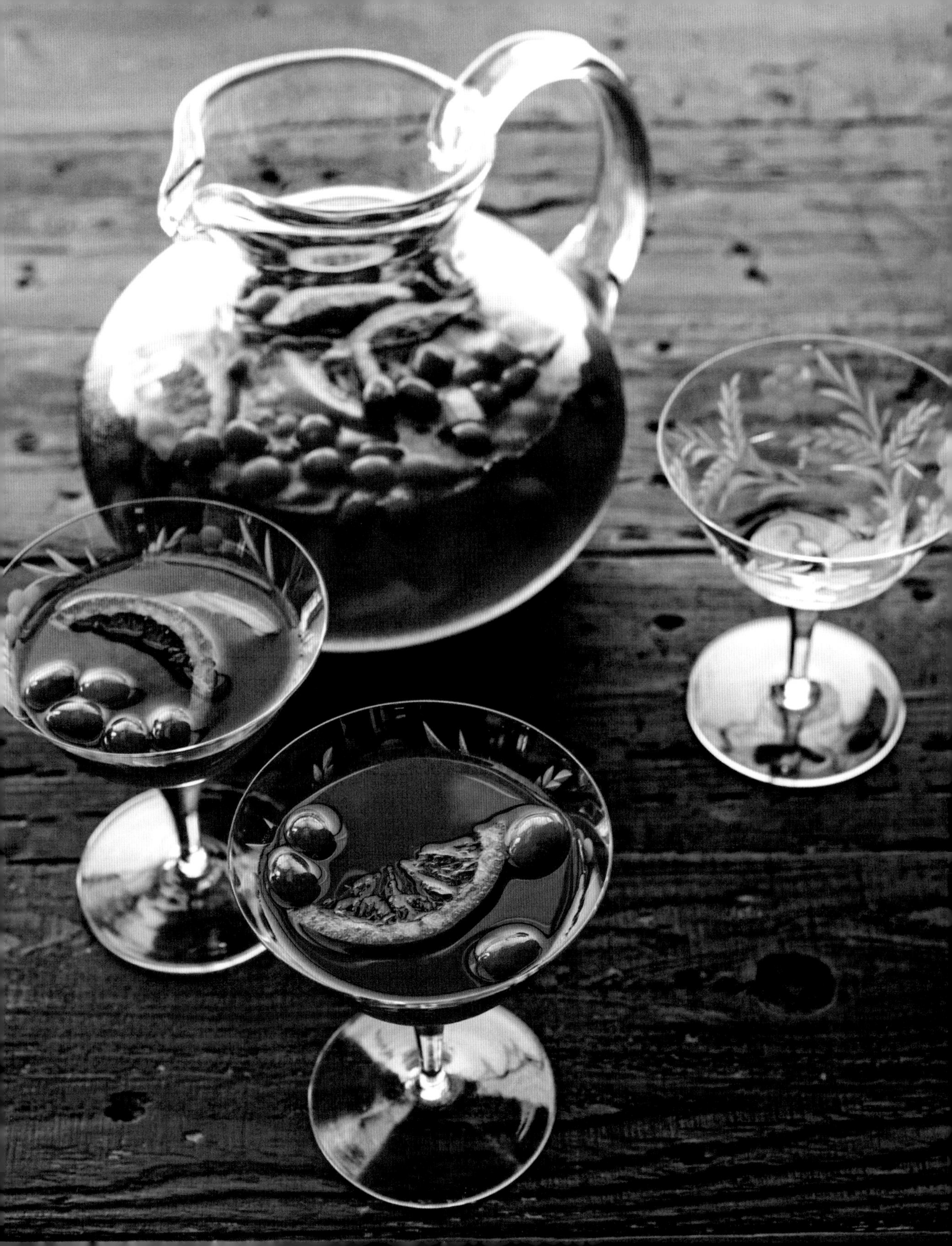

Cranberry-Spiced Apple Cider

Growing up, we had hot apple cider around Halloween; I found it comforting and it steeled me against all the ghosts and goblins.

This version contains cranberries, so it's got a Thanksgiving-Christmas vibe you can enjoy through the holiday season. And speaking of enjoying, cider is also a great drink to spike with rum or bourbon if you need even more courage.

Makes ten 6-ounce servings, or 2 quarts

2 quarts fresh-pressed apple cider
6 star anise
4 cinnamon sticks
10 allspice berries

One 12-ounce bag frozen cranberries
1 orange, cut into ¼-inch slices
One 12-ounce bag fresh cranberries,
 for parties

1. In a large saucepan over medium heat, combine the cider, star anise, cinnamon, allspice, and frozen cranberries. Bring to a boil, then reduce the heat to a simmer and cook 30 minutes.
2. Set a strainer over a large bowl and strain the cider mixture. Discard the spices and cranberries. The cider is ready to drink now, or it can be cooled completely and stored in the fridge for up to 1 week.
3. To serve, pour into a glass and float an orange slice on top.
4. For parties, transfer the cider to a slow cooker, add the fresh cranberries, and adjust the cooker to the "keep warm" setting. Add the orange slices right before guests arrive. Set out a ladle and some glasses so guests can help themselves.

Elderflower and Blackberry Spritz

Elderflower liqueur is the kind of thing I used to ignore when I saw it behind the bars at restaurants. I mean, who wants to drink *elderflower*? And then the mixology revolution came along and elderflower liqueur became all the rage, thank goodness—it's fantastic! Elderflower imparts a lovely herbal essence to a drink that clearly makes its presence known but doesn't overwhelm. A quick Google search of elderflower tells me that it has "notes of pear and lychee." Well, la-dee-da.

Makes 2 servings

½ cup frozen blackberries
8 ounces prosecco, chilled
4 ounces St.-Germain (elderflower liqueur), chilled

1 lime, cut into quarters
1 small bottle or can seltzer, chilled

1. Fill two highball glasses with ice. Divide the blackberries between the glasses.
2. Divide the prosecco and St.-Germain between the glasses. Squeeze a wedge of lime into each drink. Stir.
3. Top off each glass with seltzer. Garnish each with remaining lime wedges. Serve immediately.

Gingerbread Irish Coffee

Whoever thought up combining booze with coffee was a genius Irishman . . . who probably stayed up all night partying! This is my take on a classic drink, with a spicy, holiday twist.

Makes 2 servings

½ cup heavy cream
2 teaspoons confectioners' sugar
¼ teaspoon ground cinnamon
⅛ teaspoon ground ginger
⅛ teaspoon ground cloves

Pinch of freshly grated nutmeg
2 cups hot coffee
1 tablespoon packed brown sugar
2 to 3 ounces Irish whiskey or bourbon

1. Combine the cream, confectioners' sugar, cinnamon, ginger, cloves, and nutmeg in a medium bowl and beat with a whisk or hand mixer until soft peaks form. Set aside.

2. Divide the coffee, brown sugar, and bourbon between two tall glasses. Stir to blend. Top with the whipped cream and serve immediately.

Rosemary-Lemon Soda

Who doesn't like the combination of rosemary and lemon? It's like my chicken recipe in a glass!

Cancel that.

This is a sweet and lemony libation, with a generous pour of vodka and a rosemary twist. The recipe yields more rosemary syrup than you need for two drinks so there's more for later, when the party heats up. If you don't end up using all the syrup, it'll keep in a glass jar in the fridge for two weeks. *Makes 2 servings*

ROSEMARY SYRUP
Three 4-inch fresh rosemary sprigs
½ cup sugar

COCKTAIL
4 ounces vodka
¼ cup rosemary syrup
Juice of 2 lemons
1 small bottle or can seltzer
2 thin lemon slices
2 sprigs of rosemary

1. Make the syrup: Combine the rosemary, sugar, and ½ cup water in a small saucepan. Bring to a boil over medium-high heat and cook until the sugar is completely dissolved, about 2 minutes. Set aside to cool.
2. Fill two tall glasses with ice. Pour 2 ounces of vodka and 2 tablespoons of rosemary syrup into each glass and divide the lemon juice between the glasses. Top off with seltzer and garnish each cocktail with 1 lemon slice and a sprig of rosemary. Serve immediately.

Aperol Betty

Aperol liqueur has a bittersweet flavor that's great for drinks. Although grapefruit juice is new for me in cocktails, I've become a hardcore fan because of its combination of sweet, sour, and bitter tastes—it's a complicated fruit! Throw in some prosecco bubbles and you've got a real delight. Drink up.

Makes 2 servings

3 very thin orange slices
Superfine sugar (see "Sweet
    Confusion," page 54)
2 ounces Aperol or Campari,
    chilled

¼ cup fresh squeezed orange
    juice
¼ cup fresh squeezed
    grapefruit juice
6 ounces prosecco, chilled

1. Wipe the rims of 2 coupe glasses with one of the orange slices. Sprinkle some of the sugar in a shallow dish and dip the rims in the sugar, shaking off any excess. Set aside.
2. Fill a cocktail shaker with ice. Add the Aperol and fruit juices, and shake until beads of sweat form on the shaker. Pour into the prepared glasses.
3. Pour half of the prosecco into each glass. Float an orange slice in each cocktail. Serve immediately.

Chamomile Hot Toddy

I make this drink when I'm trying to stave off a cold; if I feel the tiniest tickle in my throat, I whip up a mug, and I always feel fine the next day. Because it contains both chamomile and bourbon, it's great for bringing on sleep. That said, you don't have to get sick—or be an insomniac—to enjoy it!

Makes 1 serving

1 chamomile teabag
3 teaspoons honey

1 ounce bourbon
Juice of ½ lemon

1. Combine 1 cup boiling water and the teabag in a mug. Let steep for 3 minutes. Discard the teabag.
2. Stir in the honey, bourbon, and lemon juice. Serve immediately.

Jalapeño-Pineapple Margarita

For sinus problems, I use this recipe. I just pour a pitcher of margaritas into a neti pot and run it through my nose.

Kidding.

This is a serious party drink. Although I'm sensitive to the kick of jalapeños (I go easy on them, so find your level), there's nothing like a few spicy margaritas to push the party up a notch. Or five. *Arriba!*

Makes 4 servings

¼ cup sugar
¼ cup unsweetened pineapple juice
¼ cup lime juice
1 jalapeño, halved (seeded, if you prefer
   a milder heat)

6 ounces tequila
3 ounces Cointreau
4 pineapple wedges

1. In a small saucepan over medium-high heat, combine the sugar, pineapple juice, lime juice, and jalapeño. Bring to a boil, then reduce the heat to low and simmer until the sugar is completely dissolved, about 2 minutes. Set aside to cool completely. Discard the jalapeño halves.
2. Fill a cocktail shaker with ice and add the pineapple syrup, tequila, and Cointreau. Shake until beads of sweat form on the shaker.
3. Fill four rocks glasses with ice cubes and divide the margarita among the glasses. Garnish with pineapple wedges and serve immediately.

YOU SALTY DOG

The margarita world divides itself between those who do and those who don't prefer a salted rim. Personally, I like them, and I've recently discovered that I can make my own "sweet" salts to make the rim even more exciting.

Here's how: Take ¼ cup freeze-dried fruit, 1 tablespoon sugar, and ¼ teaspoon sea salt and grind them finely in a spice grinder. Spread the "sweet salt" in a shallow dish. Dip the rim of a glass in lemon or lime juice (or run a wedge of either fruit along the rim), then dip the rim of the glass in the sweet salt.

Cucumber-Mint Mocktail

This drink is the definition of cool. Both mint and cucumber are naturally cooling to the body, and the crushed ice finishes the job. Perfect for a hot summer day, this drink—although easy to spike—is a thoughtful nod to your sober friends and family.

Makes 2 servings

Handful of fresh mint leaves
4 lime wedges
2 teaspoons sugar

6 cucumber slices
1 small bottle or can seltzer, ginger ale, or ginger beer

1. Divide the mint between two rocks glasses. Add 1 lime wedge and 1 teaspoon sugar to each glass. Muddle to release the lime juice and dissolve the sugar.
2. Fill the glasses with ice, preferably crushed. Tuck the cucumber slices around the sides of the glass. Top off with the seltzer. Garnish with the remaining lime wedges. Serve immediately.

See the photo on page 204.

LEFT: Cherry (Pink) Lemonade, opposite
RIGHT: Cucumber-Mint Mocktail, page 203

Cherry (Pink) Lemonade

As a little girl, I always thought pink lemonade was so . . . *cool*. And I've loved it ever since. So here's mine. By cooking down the cherries, you'll get a fantastic flavor, but you can also take the shortcut of buying cherry juice at the store.

P.S. Throw a little prosecco or champagne into half of the lemonade, and both the kids and adults will have a great time. ***Makes 6 servings, or 1¼ quarts***

¼ cup sugar
1 pint fresh sweet cherries, pitted

1 cup fresh-squeezed lemon juice
(from about 4 large lemons)

1. Combine the sugar with ¼ cup water in a small saucepan and bring to a boil over high heat. Reduce the heat and simmer until the sugar is completely dissolved, about 2 minutes. Set aside.
2. Process the cherries in a food processor until you have a smooth puree.
3. Strain the cherry puree through a fine-mesh strainer into a bowl, pressing down on the solids to extract as much cherry juice as possible. Discard the solids.
4. Combine the sugar syrup, cherry juice, and lemon juice in a large pitcher. Add 4½ cups of water, and stir until well mixed. Chill until ready to serve.

Guest Goodies

One of the great benefits of all the party planning I outlined earlier is that if you organize yourself well (and well ahead of the party) you may have time to make some guest goodies. These are little surprises you hand out at the door as people leave—think of them as the grown-up version of birthday-party grab bags, but without the bubblegum and baseball cards. These goodies are thoughtful and elegant, and yes, you're finding your inner Martha Stewart here. Of course, there will be plenty of parties for which you just don't have the time to do this stuff, but when you do . . . you'll never regret that giddy feeling of giving a guest goody.

Or . . . forget the guests! Just make these treats for yourself. They're great.

Better-Than-Almond-Roca Bark

This is a glamorous little gift—like something you'd bring back from a European vacation—but it's deceptively easy to make. Friends on their way home from your party will let this bark melt in their mouths and exclaim to their spouses: "That wath the betht pahty evah!!"

Makes about 1 quart

1½ cups slivered almonds
1 cup milk chocolate chips
½ pound (2 sticks) unsalted butter

1 cup sugar
1 teaspoon pure vanilla extract
Flaky sea salt (such as Maldon)

1. Preheat the oven to 350°F.

2. Line a 9 × 13-inch rimmed baking sheet with a piece of parchment paper long enough to hang over the sides. Spread the almonds on the sheet. Bake until golden and fragrant, 8 to 10 minutes. Measure out ½ cup of the almonds, chop them very fine, and set aside. Leave the remaining almonds on the baking sheet.

3. Pour about 1 inch of water into a small saucepan and bring it to a boil. Set a small heatproof bowl over the pot (it should fit snugly, so no steam can escape). Reduce the heat to low and pour the chocolate chips into the bowl. Let them sit, stirring occasionally, until completely melted, about 8 minutes.

4. Meanwhile, combine the butter, sugar, and vanilla in a medium saucepan over medium-high heat. Cook, tilting the pan occasionally, until the sugar and butter are completely melted (best not to stir sugar while it melts, as it will seize up and burn). Continue cooking, stirring constantly with a rubber spatula, until the mixture turns a deep golden brown—the whole process should take 15 or 16 minutes. Pour the toffee evenly over the almonds on the baking sheet. Let sit for 5 minutes.

5. Pour the chocolate over the toffee, using an offset spatula to spread it evenly. Sprinkle some salt over the chocolate, along with the reserved chopped almonds. Let cool until set, 6 hours or overnight (if your house is warm, place it in the refrigerator, uncovered). Break the bark into pieces, or cut it with a knife. (FYI, this toffee is sturdy but can crumble a bit. When you cut it, some pieces will be perfect and others less so. But don't stress—they will all be delicious.) Package in clear cellophane bags or glass jars.

Morning Granola

This is my simple, classic granola. It's sort of a base with which you can experiment. Feel free to add nuts or seeds, but if you want to use dried fruit, stir it in as soon as the granola comes out of the oven. No matter how you make it, granola is a nice gift for friends.

Makes 5 cups

3 cups old-fashioned oats (not quick cooking)
1 cup sliced almonds
1 cup unsweetened shredded coconut

Pinch of sea salt
½ cup pure maple syrup
¼ cup canola oil
1 teaspoon pure vanilla extract

1. Preheat the oven to 325°F and line an 11 × 17-inch rimmed baking sheet with parchment paper.
2. Combine the oats, almonds, coconut, and salt in a large bowl. Stir in the syrup, oil, and vanilla.
3. Spread the granola in an even layer on the prepared baking sheet. Bake for 30 minutes, stirring halfway through, until the granola is golden and fragrant.
4. Let the granola cool completely. Package in mason jars or clear cellophane bags tied with ribbon.

Milk Chocolate Sea Salt Caramels

The whole world has fallen in love with caramels and sea salt, and rightly so—their sweet and savory dynamic is fantastic. Your friends will gobble these up. . . . In fact, friends become *best* friends after eating these.

Makes 36 candies

¾ cup sugar
8 tablespoons (1 stick) unsalted butter, cut into 16 pieces
¾ cup heavy cream
½ teaspoon pure vanilla extract

½ cup milk chocolate chips
Flaky sea salt (such as Maldon)
Thirty-six 3 × 4-inch pieces of waxed paper

1. Line an 8-inch loaf pan with a piece of parchment paper long enough to hang over all the sides.
2. Pour the sugar into a heavy-bottomed 4-quart saucepan over medium-high heat. Let the sugar cook, undisturbed, until you see it begin melting around the edges, then start tilting the pot gently back and forth, letting the sugar fall onto itself, which helps it to melt evenly without burning (the handles will be hot, so use pot holders).
3. When the sugar is a golden brown and completely melted, add the butter, cream, and vanilla (it will bubble and steam up a bit). Cook, stirring constantly, for 4 minutes.
4. Take the pot off the heat momentarily and stir in the chocolate. Return to the heat and cook for 30 seconds more.
5. Pour the caramel into the prepared pan. Let set at room temperature at least 6 hours and preferably overnight.
6. Use sharp kitchen scissors to cut the caramels into 36 pieces. Wrap the caramels in the waxed paper, and package in cellophane bags or tins. They will stay fresh for up to 1 week.

TOP LEFT: Salted Dark Chocolate Truffles, page 213
TOP RIGHT: Peppermint Kisses, page 212
BOTTOM: Milk Chocolate Sea Salt Caramels, opposite

Peppermint Kisses

I never thought this Cleveland girl would bake proper meringues, but I've since learned how easy they are, and the first time I handed some to a guest, my heart just melted. The moment was as light and as sweet as the meringue! *Makes 60 kisses*

SPECIAL EQUIPMENT
pastry bag

2 large egg whites, at room temperature

⅛ teaspoon cream of tartar
½ cup sugar
¼ teaspoon peppermint extract

1. Preheat the oven to 200°F. Line an 11 × 17-inch baking sheet with parchment paper.
2. In a clean and dry large bowl, combine the egg whites and cream of tartar. With a mixer, beat on medium speed until frothy. Increase the speed to high and add the sugar in a slow, steady stream—it should take 4 to 5 minutes to add it all.
3. Continue beating the egg whites until they become stiff and glossy. Add the peppermint and beat for 30 seconds more.
4. Fill a pastry bag with the meringue mixture. Pipe bite-size drops onto the prepared pan, ¼ inch to ½ inch apart. Bake until dry and crisp, about 1½ hours. Try not to open the door during baking. Remove the baking sheet from the oven and let cool at least 15 minutes before removing the meringues from the sheet. Completely cooled meringues are best packaged in glass jars or tins and stored in a cool, dry place. They will keep for up to 3 days.

See the photo on page 211.

MAKE IT FANCY

These kisses can be garnished with finely crushed candy canes (before baking) during the holidays. Finely chopped nuts are nice, too. The peppermint extract can be swapped out with other flavors for your own spin . . . vanilla, lemon, almond. Go crazy.

Salted Dark Chocolate Truffles

The first time I ever tasted chocolate truffles was in New York City and I remember it like it was yesterday: PBS was showing the entire *eight* hours of *Nicholas Nickleby*, a huge Broadway hit at the time, and I went to a friend's apartment in the West Village to watch. It was a long and fantastic day full of champagne, Chinese food, and Dickensian drama, all topped off with chocolate truffles. The whole experience felt fancy and very . . . New York. On that day, I knew I'd found my tribe. Here's my take on a truffle that, because it contains espresso, will keep you awake for all of *Nicholas Nickleby*.   ***Makes 28 truffles***

½ cup heavy cream
2 teaspoons instant espresso powder
8 ounces dark or bittersweet
   chocolate chips

½ teaspoon pure vanilla extract
Generous pinch of sea salt
2 tablespoons unsweetened cocoa
   powder, sifted

1. Line an 8 × 4-inch loaf pan with a sheet of parchment paper long enough to cover the bottom and sides.
2. In a small saucepan over medium heat, combine the cream and espresso. Heat until the cream is very hot but not boiling.
3. Place the chocolate in a medium bowl and pour the hot cream mixture over. Let the chocolate sit, undisturbed, until it begins to melt.
4. Add the vanilla and salt and use a rubber spatula to stir until the chocolate is completely melted and smooth. Pour the mixture into the prepared pan. Chill in the fridge 45 to 60 minutes, until cooled and just firm enough to scoop (it should still be somewhat soft). If you forget and chill the mixture too long, you can let the pan sit on the counter for 10 minutes to soften it slightly.
5. Line a baking sheet with waxed paper. Scoop out the truffles using a 2-teaspoon cookie scoop and set them on the baking sheet. Chill for 30 minutes.
6. Place the cocoa powder in a small bowl. One by one, roll the truffles in the palms of your hands to form smooth balls, drop them into the cocoa power, and roll them around to coat. Place the truffles in a container in a single layer, or separate layers with sheets of waxed paper between the layers. Store the truffles at room temperature for up to 5 days.

See the photo on page 211.

Strawberry Jam

How homey is it to give a jar of jam? It smacks of love, sincerity, and *Little House on the Prairie*. Best of all, friends tell me that they think of me—and all the Emmys I've won—when they spread it on their toast in the morning.

Okay, maybe not the Emmys.

Makes two ½-pint jars

SPECIAL EQUIPMENT

Two sterilized ½-pint jars (see "How to Sterilize Glass Jars," page 85)

1 quart strawberries, hulled and chopped (roughly or finely, depending on how chunky you prefer your jam)

2 cups sugar

One 3-inch piece lemon rind (with the white pith intact—it contains pectin)

1. Two hours before you start, place a small glass dish in the freezer.

2. Place the strawberries, sugar, and lemon rind in a large saucepan (think three times the volume of the fruit). Give everything a good stir to combine. Bring the mixture to a rolling boil over high heat, using a spoon to skim the foam from the top. (Don't skip this step or you'll end up with a cloudy jam.) After a few minutes, the foam will mostly subside.

3. Lower the heat to a vigorous simmer (with bubbles constantly popping to the surface). Let the jam continue to cook for 15 to 20 minutes, until reduced by half and thick enough to generously coat a wooden spoon. At this point, you can start testing your jam for doneness. Remove the dish from the freezer and drizzle a small amount of jam on it. Tilt the dish sideways and if it holds in place without being too runny, then it's ready. The consistency will still be thin. Don't worry; the jam will thicken and set up further as it cools.

4. Spoon the hot jam into the sterilized jars. Let the jars cool completely and store in the refrigerator for up to 1 month. Be sure to write this keep-fresh date on any label or note you include with the jam. If you'd like to make jam that lasts longer, you need to use the hot-water process to seal the jars properly (Google it).

DIY Cracker Jack

Popcorn is all-American: the food of county fairs, movies, and baseball games. This is the perfect take-home gift after a BBQ or summer party. If you'd like to heat things up, add 1 teaspoon chipotle powder for a smoky caramel corn. ***Makes 8 cups***

5 tablespoons unsalted butter
⅓ cup brown rice syrup or corn syrup
⅔ cup packed dark brown sugar
½ teaspoon pure vanilla extract
¼ teaspoon baking soda

Cooking spray, for the spatula
8 cups popcorn, plain or lightly salted, but not buttered
1½ cups roasted peanuts, salted or unsalted, to your taste

1. Line two rimmed baking sheets with parchment brown paper.
2. Place the butter in a deep, microwave-safe bowl and cook in the microwave on high for 1 minute, until melted. Stir in the brown rice syrup and brown sugar and cook on high until the sugar is completely dissolved, about 2 minutes, depending on your microwave (mine is 1,000 watts).
3. Quickly stir in the vanilla extract and baking soda—it will bubble and foam up slightly. Coat a rubber spatula with cooking spray and fold in the popcorn and peanuts, trying to coat each piece. The mixture will be very sticky.
4. Cook on high power until the caramel coating begins to turn lightly golden, about 90 seconds. Carefully remove the bowl from the microwave (it will be very hot) and stir again to make sure the kernels are thoroughly coated. Cook on high until the coating turns a deeper golden color and the caramel corn starts to smell like butterscotch, 1 to 2 more minutes, watching carefully during the last 30 seconds to ensure it doesn't burn.
5. Divide the caramel corn between the prepared baking sheets and spread it into a single layer. Let it cool completely, at least 30 minutes. Break up into pieces before serving or packaging in cellophane bags for guests. The caramel corn can be also stored in an airtight tin. It will stay fresh for up to 3 days.

Best Hot Cocoa Mix

With five kids, my parents had to pinch pennies, so we would wake up to a pretty chilly house in the winter. In order to warm up, we'd sit next to the heating vents with mugs of hot cocoa. This is a simple—yet very sweet—gift to keep your guests warm after the party. *Makes 4 gift jars; each will make about 8 cups of cocoa*

SPECIAL EQUIPMENT
Four 1-pint mason jars

1½ cups cocoa powder

1 cup vanilla sugar (see "DIY Vanilla Sugar," below)
Pinch of sea salt
2 cups mini-marshmallows

1. Whisk the cocoa, sugar, and salt together in a large bowl.
2. Divide the mix among the mason jars. Top each with ½ cup marshmallows. Make labels or decorative tags for each that read: *To make hot cocoa, give the jar a shake to mix in the marshmallows, and stir 2 tablespoons of mix into 1 cup of hot milk.*

DIY VANILLA SUGAR

Give new life to used vanilla beans! When the seeds have been scraped out, tuck the pods into a jar of granulated sugar. After 1 week, the sugar will be fragrant and add a vanilla flavor to anything you use it in. No need to discard the pod; it can stay in the sugar jar indefinitely.

If you don't have time to make your own vanilla sugar, however, use granulated sugar and instruct your guests, on the label, to add a splash of vanilla extract to their cocoa right before serving.

Blueberry Shortbread Cookies

Having been married to a Brit for twenty-six years, I've become a huge fan of shortbread. Not only is it delicious, it's a safe weapon for marital disputes, since it crumbles easily upon contact with a head.

My take on shortbread uses confectioners' sugar as opposed to granulated, so the cookies come out a little sweeter and firmer. Instead of the blueberries (can you tell I love blueberries?) you can use mini chocolate chips, or nothing at all. No need to adjust the other ingredients. Jolly good!

Makes 18 cookies

½ pound (2 sticks) unsalted butter, softened
⅔ cup confectioners' sugar
¼ teaspoon pure vanilla or almond extract, optional

¼ teaspoon sea salt
2 cups all-purpose flour, plus more for rolling
¼ cup plus 2 tablespoons dried blueberries

1. Preheat the oven to 350°F. Line an 11 × 17-inch baking sheet with parchment paper.
2. Combine the butter, sugar, and extract (if using) in a large bowl and beat until creamy and a bit fluffy, 3 to 5 minutes.
3. Beat in the salt. Add the flour in ½-cup increments on low speed, adding more flour as it absorbs into the butter mixture. The dough will seem crumbly and almost too soft—don't worry. Sprinkle in the dried blueberries. Gather it into a ball and very gently knead it once or twice.
4. On a lightly floured counter, roll out the dough to a ¼-inch thickness. Press out circles with a 2½-inch cutter. Transfer the circles to the prepared baking sheet and bake 15 to 17 minutes, until barely golden around the edges. Let the cookies cool completely on the baking sheet (they will crisp up as they cool) before packaging in cellophane bags for your guests. If you're keeping them for yourself, store them in a cookie tin, in a cool, dry place.

DROP THAT COOKIE

If you don't feel like rolling out the dough, you can make drop cookies by using a 1½-teaspoon cookie dough scoop and baking for 15 minutes. This will make 30 cookies.

Infused Sea Salts

I'm a big salt person. Until I discovered how to make my own, I bought infused salts all the time, but now I experiment with different flavors in my own kitchen. Most salts are used for finishing—over salads, on freshly cooked vegetables, or in soups. A lime salt would be particularly wonderful on fresh chunks of watermelon. An orangy salt would be a nice surprise on seafood, where people usually pair lemon. Herbed salts (think hardy herbs such as rosemary, thyme, or oregano) would be fun for popcorn as well as savory dishes.

I encourage you to give this recipe a try; it will make you look like a combination of Julia Child and Martha Stewart . . . which would make you a very tall billionaire, I guess.

Not bad.

Finally, this is the kind of thing that people will actually use, and the essence of your party—and your spirit—will carry on. You can't go wrong with this.   ***Makes ½ cup***

½ cup flaky sea salt (such as Maldon)

1 tablespoon citrus zest, finely chopped fresh herbs, or a combination of both

1. Preheat the oven to 225°F and line a rimmed baking sheet with parchment paper.
2. Combine the salt and zest in a medium bowl. Use your fingers to mix well, rubbing the zest into the salt and making sure there aren't any clumps of zest. Spread the salt on the prepared baking sheet. (If making a few different varieties, just section them into rows—no need to use multiple pans.)
3. Bake for 70 minutes, or until the citrus is completely dried out (it should crumble when rubbed between your fingers). Set the baking sheet on a wire rack to cool.
4. You can leave the salt in larger flakes and package in small jars (a little goes a long way), or pulse it a few times in a food processor for a finer grain before packaging. Package into small resealable bags. The salts will keep in an airtight container, stored in a cool, dark place, for up to 6 months.

LEAVE A NOTE

While the salt is baking, consider making little note cards to include with the gift, suggesting how your guests can use their new salt at home.

Lemon, Honey, and Thyme Financiers

Financiers are a traditional French pastry made with almond flour and lots of butter, cooked in little rectangular molds that make them look like small bars of gold—hence the name. Here, I've used the financier dough for mini-muffins, which are perfect for teatime the day after your party. ***Makes 22 to 24 financiers***

Cooking spray for the muffin tins
8 tablespoons (1 stick) unsalted butter
¼ cup honey, preferably a creamy churned variety
4 large egg whites (save the yolks for another use)
½ cup all-purpose flour, plus more for the muffin pans

1 cup almond flour
1⅓ cups confectioners' sugar, plus more for dusting
1 teaspoon freshly chopped thyme leaves
½ teaspoon sea salt
Zest of 2 lemons

1. Preheat the oven to 375°F. Generously coat two 12-cup mini-muffin pans with cooking spray.
2. In a small saucepan over medium-low heat, heat the butter until it turns a deep golden color and little browned bits begin to appear, 7 to 8 minutes. (Foam will rise to the top of the pot during the browning process; these are the milk solids. Give the pot a swirl and you'll notice the foaming will dissipate as the solids begin to brown.)
3. Whisk the honey into the pan and set aside to cool slightly.
4. In a large bowl, whisk the egg whites until foamy, 30 to 60 seconds. Stir in the flours, sugar, thyme, salt, and zest, until just combined. The batter will be quite thick.
5. Gently fold in the butter mixture with a rubber spatula.
6. Spoon 1 heaping tablespoon of batter into each well of the prepared muffin tins. Bake 12 to 14 minutes, until deeply golden around the edges. Let the cakes sit in the pan on a wire rack for 10 minutes, then transfer them from the pan to the rack and let cool completely. Dust with confectioners' sugar, if desired, just before packaging.

Chocolate Streusel Pumpkin Mini-Muffins

Who doesn't want to wake up to a mini-muffin the day after your fabulous party? These babies bring together pumpkin—a personal fave—and chocolate streusel. Mmm . . .

Makes 24 mini-muffins

CHOCOLATE STREUSEL TOPPING
½ cup all-purpose flour
2 tablespoons brown sugar
1 tablespoon granulated sugar
1½ teaspoons unsweetened cocoa powder
Pinch of sea salt
3 tablespoons unsalted butter, melted

MUFFINS
1¼ cups all-purpose flour
⅓ cup packed brown sugar

3 tablespoons granulated sugar
½ teaspoon ground cinnamon
½ teaspoon ground allspice
½ teaspoon baking powder
¼ teaspoon baking soda
¼ teaspoon sea salt
Zest of 1 orange
Juice from ½ orange (¼ cup)
2 large eggs
½ cup canned pumpkin puree
¼ cup canola or vegetable oil
Confectioners' sugar, optional

1. Preheat the oven to 375°F. Line two 12-cup mini-muffin tins with paper liners.
2. Make the streusel: Whisk together the flour, sugars, cocoa, salt, and melted butter in a medium bowl. Set aside.
3. Make the muffins: Whisk together the flour, sugars, cinnamon, allspice, baking powder, baking soda, and salt. Add the orange zest and juice, eggs, pumpkin, and oil and whisk until just mixed, with no visible signs of flour.
4. Spoon the batter into the prepared muffin tins. Divide the streusel among the muffins. Bake for 9 to 10 minutes, until the muffins spring back when tapped lightly. Set the tins on a wire rack and cool completely.
5. Dust the muffins with confectioners' sugar, if desired, then package in clear cellophane bags.

Coffee-Glazed Date-Nut Bundt Cakes

I once had an assistant with amazing tattoos, and she made a bourbon-soaked Bundt cake that was out of this world. So this is my homage to tatted-out Julie. Thanks a Bundts!

Makes 6 personal-size Bundt cakes or 12 muffins

BATTER
2 cups chopped dates
1 cup 2% or whole milk
¼ cup molasses
4 tablespoons (½ stick) unsalted butter
2 cups all-purpose flour
2 teaspoons baking powder
½ teaspoon ground cinnamon
½ teaspoon sea salt
½ teaspoon ground cloves
1 large egg

½ cup sugar
1 teaspoon pure vanilla extract
1 cup toasted walnuts, chopped
    (see "Toasting Nuts," page 43)

ICING
1 cup confectioners' sugar
1½ tablespoons brewed espresso or
    coffee
1 tablespoon unsalted butter, melted
¼ teaspoon pure vanilla extract

1. Preheat the oven to 375°F. Grease and generously flour two 6-cup mini Bundt pans or line a 12-cup muffin tin with paper liners.

2. Make the batter: In a medium saucepan over medium-low heat, combine the dates, milk, molasses, and butter. Cook just until the milk is hot and the butter is melted. Remove from the heat, and set side.

3. In a medium bowl, whisk together the flour, baking powder, cinnamon, salt, and cloves. Set aside.

4. In a large bowl, combine the egg, sugar, and vanilla. Whisk vigorously until well blended. Add the milk and flour mixtures and stir just until combined. Gently stir in the walnuts.

5. Divide the batter evenly between the prepared pans. Bake until the cakes bounce back when tapped lightly and a skewer inserted comes out clean, 17 to 19 minutes for mini Bundt cakes and 15 to 17 minutes for muffins. Set the pans on a wire rack to cool completely. Turn them out after they are completely cool.

6. Make the glaze: In a medium bowl, combine the confectioners' sugar, espresso, butter, and vanilla. Whisk until smooth and drizzle over the cooled cakes. Let the cakes sit undisturbed for about 1 hour, or until the icing is set, before packaging.

Sample Menus

HERE ARE SOME RECIPE COMBINATIONS THAT ARE
DELICIOUS, FUN, AND SATISFYING . . .

Summer Party

Cherry (Pink) Lemonade   PAGE 205

A Glorious Cheese Board   PAGE 79

Roast Chicken, Tomato, and
Mozzarella Panzanella   PAGE 55

Raspberry-Lemon Icebox Cake   PAGE 174

Busy Weeknight

Cucumber-Mint Mocktail   PAGE 203

Lemon and Rosemary Roasted Chicken   PAGE 126

Warm Quinoa, Shiitake, and Feta Salad   PAGE 138

Raspberry Yogurt Ice Pops   PAGE 162

Family Gathering

Rosemary-Lemon Soda   PAGE 197

Grilled Romaine Hearts with Scallion Cream   PAGE 146

Mom's Meatballs   PAGE 95

Stuffed Shells   PAGE 121

Polenta, Pine Nut, and Rosemary Olive Oil Cake   PAGE 181

Game Day

Jalapeño-Pineapple Margarita   PAGE 200

Epic Sheet Pan Nachos   PAGE 83

Buffalo Cauliflower Bites
with Ranch Dipping Sauce   PAGE 73

Cherry Cola Sheet Cake   PAGE 182

Weekend Brunch

Elderflower and Blackberry Spritz PAGE 193

Spinach and Cheese Strata PAGE 56

Spicy Baked Avocado Eggs PAGE 45

Lemon, Honey, and Thyme Financiers PAGE 224

Date Night

Maple-Bourbon Old-Fashioned PAGE 189

Bite-Size Crab Cakes with Lemon Aioli PAGE 76

*Skillet Steak with Red Wine Sauce
and Mushrooms* PAGE 130

Peppermint Kisses PAGE 212

or Salted Dark Chocolate Truffles PAGE 213

Birthday Party

BBQ Beef Sliders PAGE 65

Classic Mac 'n' Cheese PAGE 157

DIY Cracker Jack PAGE 214

Toasted Marshmallow Milk Shake PAGE 177

(stick a candle in the whipped cream—a unique idea instead of birthday cake)

Great Dishes to Bring to a Potluck

Chutney Deviled Eggs PAGE 87

Summer Peach Hand Pies PAGE 184

Roasted Butternut Squash and Garlic Dip PAGE 85

A Glorious Cheese Board PAGE 79

Resources

We've come a long way since my mother and her red shopping wagon, and in this digital age, the world gets smaller by the minute. So if your local retailers don't have everything you need, try these:

Amazon
This giant has everything you could ever dream up and more.
www.amazon.com

D'Artagnan
Rare meats, charcuterie, and gift boxes.
www.dartagnan.com

Etsy
Don't forget Etsy, for cute, crafted goods from creative owners. Great for gifts.
www.etsy.com

Kalustyan's
Has everything you need—and didn't know you needed—for making Indian foods. A real delight.
www.kalustyans.com

La Tienda
Any food you'd ever want from Spain.
www.tienda.com

Michaels
Art supplies for centerpieces and decorations.
www.michaels.com

Mouth: Tasty Gifts from Indie Makers
This fun online store has a really amazing range of party foods and original things. Check it out.
www.mouth.com

Murray's Cheese
Based out of New York City, Murray's has an actual cheese cave.
www.murrayscheese.com

Oh Happy Day
A very cute online party shop, full of great ideas.
www.ohhappyday.com

Paper Presentation
Funky invitations and paper products.
www.paperpresentation.com

Paper Source
Gorgeous stationery for invitations.
www.papersource.com

Zingerman's Deli
In Ann Arbor, Michigan, Zingerman's is known for truly authentic imported ingredients, like olive oil.
www.zingermans.com

Acknowledgments

I'd like to thank Adam Griffin and Ryan Bundra for getting this dough ball rolling. Without you, these lovely projects would not come to life. Thanks to Jessica Porter for organizing my thoughts on paper, and to Jennifer Perillo for helping to develop my recipes.

I have deep gratitude for Ed Anderson and his fabulous photography, and to Valerie Aikman-Smith, who styled the food so well I want to lick each page! Ricci DeMartino and Jennifer Barguiarena did a fantastic job putting together the look and style for the lifestyle shots, and made us all look like supermodels.

Kudos to my literary agent, Katherine Latshaw, who brought all the pieces of this project together, and to Cassie Jones and the team at William Morrow/HarperCollins for seeing my vision and bringing it to the world. Thank you so much.

Most of all, I'd like to thank my family, who have sat at the dinner table through all the victories and defeats and still say, "Love you, Mom!"

Universal Conversion Chart

Oven temperature equivalents

250°F = 120°C

275°F = 135°C

300°F = 150°C

325°F = 160°C

350°F = 180°C

375°F = 190°C

400°F = 200°C

425°F = 220°C

450°F = 230°C

475°F = 240°C

500°F = 260°C

Measurement equivalents

Measurements should always be level unless directed otherwise.

⅛ teaspoon = 0.5 mL

¼ teaspoon = 1 mL

½ teaspoon = 2 mL

1 teaspoon = 5 mL

1 tablespoon = 3 teaspoons = ½ fluid ounce = 15 mL

2 tablespoons = ⅛ cup = 1 fluid ounce = 30 mL

4 tablespoons = ¼ cup = 2 fluid ounces = 60 mL

5⅓ tablespoons = ⅓ cup = 3 fluid ounces = 80 mL

8 tablespoons = ½ cup = 4 fluid ounces = 120 mL

10⅔ tablespoons = ⅔ cup = 5 fluid ounces = 160 mL

12 tablespoons = ¾ cup = 6 fluid ounces = 180 mL

16 tablespoons = 1 cup = 8 fluid ounces = 240 mL

Index

Note: Page references in *italics* indicate photographs.